# What on Earth is a Mainframe?

## An Introduction to IBM zSeries Mainframes and z/OS Operating System for Total Beginners

David Stephens

Long pela

Copyright © 2008 by David Stephens

All rights reserved.

First Edition: October 2008

ISBN 978-1-4092-2535-5

Order this book online at www.longpelaexpertise.com.au/books


**Produced by Longpela Expertise**

Longpela Expertise provides Mainframe Systems Programming consulting services. Find out more at

www.longpelaexpertise.com.au


Cover image of IBM z990 Processor courtesy of IBM Archives.

## Acknowledgements

You can't write a book without help from a lot of people. So here they are:

- Paul Norris for having the patience to wade through my first draft.
- Andrew Binnie for his thoughts early on.
- IBM, Xerox, Sun StorageTek, Jolly Giant software and Patrick Finnegan for supplying images.
- Hecate Jay for copy-editing a book on a topic she had absolutely no interest in.
- Mark Beckham, Brian Breathnach, Dave Matoe and Louise Wilson for reviewing the book at the end.

And special thanks to my partner Simone, who put up with me babbling on and on about this book for months.

# Contents

Contents .................................................................................. 5

Introduction ............................................................................ 9

**Chapter 1: But Aren't Mainframes Dead? An Introduction to the Mainframe ........................................................... 11**

    What is a Mainframe? _____ 11

    So If Mainframes Are So Good, Why Does Everyone Want to Get Rid of Them? _____ 14

    Why Keep Mainframes? _____ 16

    The Last Word _____ 20

**Chapter 2: What Are All These Refrigerators? Mainframe Hardware ................................................................................ 21**

    The Brains of the Organization - The Processor _____ 22

    Why Can't They Just Call Them Disks? _____ 27

    You mean Mainframes are still using TAPE? _____ 31

    Other Removable Media _____ 36

    Printers _____ 37

    Connecting the Boxes – Channels _____ 38

    What Are Environmentals? _____ 40

    The Last Word _____ 41

**Chapter 3: The z/OS Jigsaw Puzzle - The Many Pieces of z/OS ................................................................................... 43**

    What You Get When You Buy z/OS _____ 43

    12 Things You Need To Know About z/OS _____ 46

    What You Don't Get When You Buy z/OS _____ 56

    The Last Word _____ 63

## Chapter 4: Talking to z/OS - Networks and Communications ............................................................. 65

SNA Networks _____ 65
TCP/IP Networks _____ 72
Talking Between Applications – Middleware and SOA _____ 76
The Last Word _____ 80

## Chapter 5: Putting the Mainframe to Work - Database and Transaction Managers ......................................... 81

The Database Manager – Your Database Nanny _____ 81
The Transaction Manager – Crowd Management _____ 87
Transaction and Database Managers on z/OS _____ 91
Other Transaction and Database Managers _____ 107
Do I Really Need to Buy This Stuff? _____ 108
The Last Word _____ 108

## Chapter 6: Application Development on z/OS ................... 109

What's an Application? _____ 109
What's an Application Environment? _____ 110
How to Create an Application Program _____ 110
How to Develop an Application _____ 113
Supporting an Existing Application _____ 117
Why Your Source Code is Important _____ 120
Why Is It So Hard To Develop Mainframe Applications? _____ 121
Application Development Gadgets and Goodies _____ 122
The Last Word _____ 124

## Chapter 7: Accessorize - Software for the Mainframe .. 125

Monitoring Tools _____ 125
Tape Management Software _____ 129
Reporting Tools _____ 130
Output Management Software _____ 130
Software for a Disaster _____ 131

Performance Software ........... 131
Decision Support Software ........... 132
File Transfer Software ........... 132
Printing Software ........... 132
Other Goodies on the Market ........... 133
The Last Word ........... 133

## *Chapter 8: What Do All These People DO? People You Need to Run a Mainframe..........135*

Operators ........... 135
Operations Analysts ........... 138
Security Administrators ........... 139
Application Developers ........... 140
Application Testers ........... 141
Database Administrators ........... 142
Systems Programmers ........... 143
Other People ........... 146
The Last Word ........... 148

## *Chapter 9: Mainframe Manager Nightmares ........... 149*

What Do You Mean It's Unavailable? ........... 149
Where Does All the Money Go? ........... 153
Who's Paying for All of This? ........... 153
Software and Hardware Support ........... 155
Being Ready for a Disaster ........... 156
Mainframe People – Where Do I Get One? ........... 158
Paying Someone Else to Do It ........... 158
Why Is It Taking So Long? ........... 159
When Do We Get a New One? ........... 160
Providing the Mainframe With a Good Home ........... 161
Keeping it Safe ........... 161
The Last Word ........... 162

*Chapter 10: The Last Word*................................................................. *163*

*Appendix 1: An Executive Summary - The Whole Book in Three Pages* ............................................................................ *165*

*Appendix 2: Where to Go to Next* ..................................................... *169*

    IBM Redbooks™ _____ 169

    Manuals _____ 170

    Other Information on the Web _____ 170

    Magazines and Articles _____ 170

    Software Vendors _____ 171

    Hardware Vendors and Resellers _____ 173

*Appendix 3: Glossary - Translating the Mainframe Speak* ................................................................................................. *175*

*Notices* ............................................................................................. *193*

*Index* ............................................................................................... *197*

*Table of Figures* .............................................................................. *205*

*About the Author* ............................................................................ *207*

# Introduction

With an eerie creak, the long unused door succumbs to the pressure of your sweating hand and reluctantly grants you access. You take a few nervous steps into the darkness, leaving footprints on the dusty, neglected floor. As your eyes adjust to the dim light, you identify the large boxes that emit the low hum emanating from the room. Boxes that you and everyone you work with need to survive. But the people who built these boxes, who created the complex systems are now gone - long gone. And as your eyes slowly take in the contents of that dark, foreboding computer room, you wonder how on earth you're going to keep them running.

To many people who are thrown for the first time at the Mainframe beast, it can feel exactly like this. You feel like Alice entering Wonderland, and it's not a nice place. What's more IBM® and the other Mainframe people don't make life any easier. The hardware is a complete mystery, everything is done differently to any other computer on the planet, and Mainframe people seem to speak a completely different language. And what's worse, every book and manual you pick up is incredibly hard to read, and just ... so ... BORING. Where's the "Mainframe for Beginners" book? Right here.

This book is for that brave adventurer who's jumping off the precipice into the world of IBM Mainframes. It's a Beginner's Guide to the IBM® zSeries® computers and the operating system that runs on almost all of them: IBM z/OS®.

So what's covered in this book? We introduce you to the Mainframe: the hardware, the operating systems, and where a Mainframe 'sits' inside an organization's computing environment. We talk about the application and database systems that run on it, the little known accessories that are offered by IBM and other companies, and some of the issues that are important in the Mainframe world. We'll also talk about the people that work on the Mainframes: what they do, and what training they need.

Who's the book for? Absolutely everyone: new and experienced computer programmers, managers, recruitment consultants, journalists, and even friends and family of Mainframe users. In fact anyone who has anything to do with Mainframes will love this book. You don't have to know anything about Mainframes - if you can use a personal computer, then this book is for you.

This book isn't meant as a comprehensive manual on how to use or program a Mainframe. It is a brief introduction to the world of Mainframes. We have tried to write a book that is not only clear and simple to understand, but also fun to read. You can read this book cover to cover like a novel; use it as a reference, or both.

Throughout the book, we'll often be talking about "the Mainframe" by which we mean the IBM zSeries Mainframes – or the older equivalent platforms: System/370™ and System/390®. We'll also talk about z/OS - meaning the z/OS operating system and its other names: MVS® and OS/390®.

So buckle up, and let's get into it.

# Chapter 1: But Aren't Mainframes Dead? An Introduction to the Mainframe

So what exactly are these Mainframes that everyone's talking about? Let's find out...

## What is a Mainframe?

It's a big computer. In the 1970s and 1980s when almost all computers were big, the term *Mainframe* was used to refer to a number of different computer systems. Today most of these are gone, and *Mainframe* almost always refers to IBM's zSeries computers. And that's what this book is all about. From now on when we talk about Mainframes, we're talking about the zSeries.

The zSeries computers are amongst the largest computers sold today, and they're used for *commercial data processing*. By commercial data processing we're really talking about database based applications; putting a piece of data into a database, looking at it, and taking it out. Now this sounds ridiculously simple, but it's not. When you're running big database applications, you need to think about:

- **Data integrity:** My data HAS to be right – all the time.
- **Throughput:** I need to run lots and lots of work – now.
- **Response**: I want the answers NOW – not in one minute's time

- **Disaster Recovery**: If a disaster strikes, I want to be back up and running. Fast.
- **Usability**: It has to do what I want, when I want – oh yeah, and make it easy to use.
- **Reliability**: Don't tell me there's a computer problem – I want it available when I need it.
- **Audit**: I need to be able to find out who's done what in the past.
- **Security**: Only those who should, can.

So now commercial data processing is starting to sound a bit more complicated isn't it?

Today every business wanting to use computers commercially faces these issues. The individual needs, size, and business complexity will be different; but these basic issues will be there. And there are lots of computing systems and software around that can help with all this. So why do people move to a Mainframe?

Simple: they don't. There aren't many organizations that will install a Mainframe from scratch (unless they're installing Linux™ on the zSeries – this is a growing market) – and we'll discuss why soon. But the fact is that almost all Mainframe users have been using Mainframes for years (well, decades actually). People often call them *legacy* systems.

Now, the bottom line is that Mainframes do commercial data processing well. But there are things they're not good at. Things like:

- **Number crunching**. You won't find many scientific applications for the zSeries. There are cheaper, easier options out there.
- **Graphics and Geographical Information Systems**. No games like Half-Life® running on Mainframes.
- **Look good**. Let's talk about this for a second. You're familiar with Microsoft® Windows®; the mouse and the nice, fancy screens right? Well Mainframes have none of that. To talk to a Mainframe you need a 3270 terminal (a *dumb* terminal – no

processing is done here), or a PC running software that *pretends* to be a dumb terminal (3270 *emulation software*).

These dumb terminals are *character based* - have a look at Figure 1. No windows, no graphics (well, you can – but almost no-one does) - just text. People often call them *green screens*, because in the old days they had green writing on a black background. There are certainly applications connecting to the Mainframe that look good – but you'll find that all the nice, pretty stuff is done on a different computing platform.

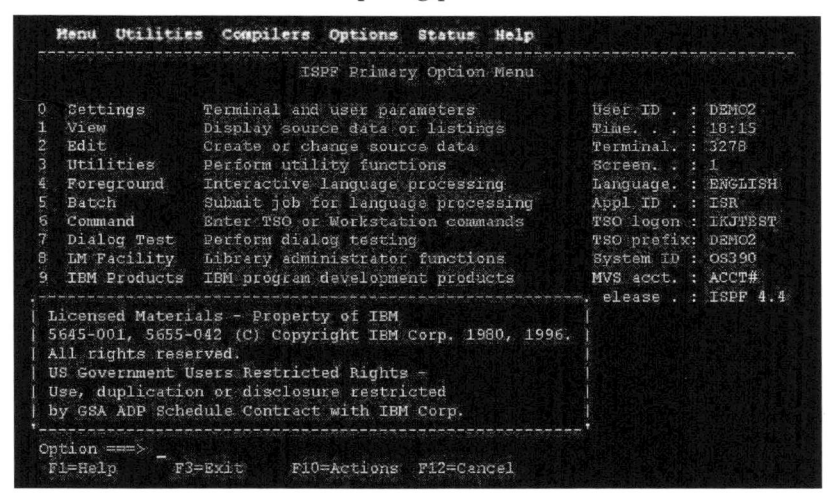

```
Menu  Utilities  Compilers  Options  Status  Help
------------------------------------------------------------
                      ISPF Primary Option Menu
 0  Settings       Terminal and user parameters      User ID . : DEMO2
 1  View           Display source data or listings   Time. . . : 18:15
 2  Edit           Create or change source data      Terminal. : 3278
 3  Utilities      Perform utility functions         Screen. . : 1
 4  Foreground     Interactive language processing   Language. : ENGLISH
 5  Batch          Submit job for language processing Appl ID . : ISR
 6  Command        Enter TSO or Workstation commands TSO logon : IKJTEST
 7  Dialog Test    Perform dialog testing            TSO prefix: DEMO2
 8  LM Facility    Library administrator functions   System ID : OS390
 9  IBM Products   IBM program development products  MVS acct. : ACCT#
                                                     elease . : ISPF 4.4
| Licensed Materials - Property of IBM              |
| 5645-001, 5655-042 (C) Copyright IBM Corp. 1980, 1996. |
| All rights reserved.                              |
| US Government Users Restricted Rights -           |
| Use, duplication or disclosure restricted         |
| by GSA ADP Schedule Contract with IBM Corp.       |

Option ===>  _
   F1=Help      F3=Exit       F10=Actions  F12=Cancel
```

**Figure 1: A 3270 Mainframe Screen** *(courtesy Jolly Giant Software)*

So congratulations! You are now the owner of a huge company (complete with private jet and corporate limousine) that for the past 20 years or so has been developing programs that run on the Mainframe. You've spent huge – no, *enormous* amounts of money, time and effort to get them working for you. So after 20 years of debugging, tweaking, changing and modifying, your Mainframe programs are working fine. But more importantly, your business for the past 20 years has been evolving around these programs. So the Mainframe has slowly become the core of your entire business. No Mainframe, no business. Welcome to the Mainframe world!

That's what most Mainframe users are facing. They've got these core systems running on Mainframes (like your bank account details), and they desperately, desperately need them.

## So If Mainframes Are So Good, Why Does Everyone Want to Get Rid of Them?

There must be hundreds of computing journalists today that see the zSeries Mainframe as a computing Rasputin. Shoot him, poison him, drown him – and somehow he still keeps breathing! For many years computer magazines have delighted in writing about the death of zSeries Mainframes - and many people believed them (and still do). But why don't people like them? And why aren't there many new Mainframe users? Simple: money, people, internet.

### *Money*

Mainframes are expensive - very expensive. And we're not just talking about buying the Mainframe hardware and software. You're also up for:

- Hardware support costs – if they break, you need someone to come and fix them.
- Software licensing costs – the right to run the software, and support in case there's a problem with it.
- People to look after and maintain the Mainframe.
- A computer room - you can't put a Mainframe under your desk. They need an air-conditioned, climate controlled computer room.

IBM has worked hard in recent years to reduce the costs of Mainframes and they've been quite successful. But the fact remains that Mainframes still aren't cheap.

## People

Mainframes are far harder to look after than other computing options. Let's look at this for a second:

- You need more people to look after a Mainframe.

- Mainframes are harder to use, so these people need to have more training. A typical University graduate can administer a UNIX® server without a great deal of training. The same graduate needs a couple of years training to become a competent Mainframe administrator.

- You can't find people who are Mainframe-savvy. Quality people with Mainframe skills or skills in programming older languages like COBOL are becoming harder to find. Few University graduates become skilled on the Mainframe, and existing Mainframe experts are slowly retiring. We talk more about this later.

## Internet

Picture this: you've got all this data and lots of programs that access, process and change it. But Mainframes aren't pretty, and you want pretty applications. Applications that let people get to your data from the internet and intranets. Applications that can make it look nice: drop down boxes, fancy graphics - the works.

Now Mainframes in the past haven't played well with other systems. In past years if you wanted to connect your Mainframe system to the internet it was hard, if not impossible.

IBM has made a lot of changes to the Mainframe to fix this. For example, z/OS includes UNIX. That's right - a full, complete UNIX operating system is inside z/OS. This certainly means that you can run UNIX applications under z/OS. But perhaps more importantly this gives you a path between your older Mainframe applications and UNIX oriented programs and equipment, including the internet. Nonetheless, connecting your Mainframe applications with newer systems and technology still isn't a straightforward task.

So, that sounds pretty convincing doesn't it? Bring over that dump truck — we're getting rid of all our Mainframes! But before we start looking for extra large garbage bags, let's have a look at the other side.

> ### IBM as Snow White? The Mainframe Market Today
>
> If you were in the market for a computer in the 1950s and 1960s, you were looking at Mainframes - there was really nothing else. And the dominant player was IBM.
>
> The Mainframe market in those days was sometimes called 'IBM and the Seven Dwarfs' - the 'dwarfs' being the other major Mainframe manufacturers: Burroughs, Control Data, General Electric, Honeywell, NCR, RCA, and UNIVAC.
>
> In many ways the Mainframe market today hasn't changed much - a dominant IBM together with manufacturers such as:
>
> - Fujitsu Siemens® BS2000 running OSD.
> - Fujitsu® Trimetra NOVA running Open/VME (originally ICL VME).
> - HP NonStop server (originally Tandem NonStop).
> - Unisys ClearPath running MCP (originally Burroughs) and OS220 (originally Univac-Sperry).
> - Bull NovaScale 9000 Series running GCOS 8.
>
> All of these systems are still in use today, and are being fully supported by their vendors. Like the zSeries they are legacy systems (meaning they're old technology but still needed), and most have been developed so they can also run UNIX, and in some cases even Microsoft® Windows®.
>
> Users of these Mainframes are faced with many of the same issues as zSeries Mainframe users — high costs, web-enablement, future development, future support, and finding skilled technical people.

# Why Keep Mainframes?

Here's an interesting fact - the amount of work Mainframes are doing around the world is *increasing*. That's right, though the number of Mainframes being used has dropped over the past years, if you add up all the processing they do — it's increasing. In fact, you will find that most major banks, insurance companies, and larger government departments in more industrialized countries have a Mainframe or two hidden in the computer room closet. So why haven't they moved on? Two reasons: it's hard to move, and Mainframes do some things better.

## It's Hard to Move Away From Mainframes

Remember? You're the owner of that organization that first invested in Mainframes 20 years ago? All the Mainframe programs and systems have been evolving to suit your business. And what's more, your business has been evolving around the Mainframe. You're joined at the hip. The Mainframe and its applications are the core of your business — holding the critical information. You simply cannot do without the functionality or the data.

> ### The Y2K 'Bug' – A Mainframe Disease
>
> In the 1990s, the Y2K 'bug' made worldwide headlines. Many were predicting catastrophic problems on January 1, 2000 for older applications – especially those running on Mainframes.
>
> This was caused by many older applications using just two digits to store the year. For example, 1999 was stored as '99'. So in 2000, some applications would think that it was 1900.
>
> Many organizations were facing the huge cost of changing their older mainframe applications – and decided not to. Instead, they spent their money on moving their applications away from the mainframe.

So to move away from the Mainframe you have to:

- Buy new hardware – and this hardware needs to be as reliable as the Mainframe hardware.

- Buy new systems software – and this needs to be reliable too.

- Find people who can administer your new systems.

- Create new procedures to administer your new systems. For example: backups, database maintenance, security, audit, and Disaster Recovery.

- Either rewrite all your programs (that you've spent 20 years developing and modifying) on another platform and in another language, or modify an 'off the shelf package' - software already written. And it had all better work.

- Train all your users to use the new system.

- Migrate all your data from the Mainframe to the newer system.

- Find something to do with all the Mainframe people that are now out of a job.

Also remember that you need to cutover from your old system to a new one. So you're going to have to shutdown the Mainframe systems, migrate your existing data across, then startup the new system – and hope it works.

Oh yes, we almost forgot about cost – none of this is going to be cheap. So you're going to need a very good reason to make this change.

There are many cases where organizations have attempted this and failed. Or migrated only half of their systems. Or migrated to a new system that is slower, crashes regularly, and doesn't do everything the old system did. But there are also many cases where a migration from a Mainframe application to a different system has been incredibly successful – just what was needed. Either way there's no doubting that it's hard to do, will cost a lot, and can be risky.

## *Mainframes Do Some Things Better*

Think about ambulances. If you're running an ambulance service are you going to buy cheap or used vehicles to use as ambulances? No way! You're going to want to spend money on vehicles that you know won't break down. And what's more, you're going to want to spend lots of money looking after and maintaining those vehicles because if they fail, people die.

In many cases, the Mainframe is like this (except that no-one dies). Yes, it's a system based on older technology. But in some ways it is the best at what it does. Its strengths are:

- **Reliability**: Would you believe that the 'z' in zSeries stands for 'zero downtime?' Although this is a bit of marketing, there's no doubt that Mainframes run, and run, and run.

  Mainframe hardware is the most reliable on the planet – and the best supported. If it breaks, you'll have an engineer at your doorstep in a flash, 24 hours a day. Mainframe software has been used for the critical business applications of many large corporations for many years. Today, an organization with a properly setup and run Mainframe can measure the time between unscheduled outages in YEARS.

- **Accountability**: The z/OS operating system has the best recording of any operating system on the planet. This recording has little overhead, and lets you monitor everything from performance (how fast did we do that?), to security (who tried to do that?), and accounting (who and how much do we charge for that?)

---

### Why Are Mainframes Using Older Technology?

So why are Mainframes using old technology - why can't they simply use new technology as it becomes available? Because of *Backward Compatibility*.

In 1964, IBM released a new Mainframe - the System/360. But there was one problem - the System/360 wouldn't run programs written on the previous IBM machines - so customers had to rewrite them. The System/360™ (now z/Series) almost bankrupted IBM.

Today, every time a new Mainframe is released it has to work with existing mainframe application programs and software - it has to be *backward compatible*. This makes it a little more difficult for IBM to move to newer technology.

---

- **Data integrity**: Yes, we're back to this. When data integrity is important you can't beat the Mainframe. The database applications that run on z/OS such as IMS and DB2 have lots of features to make sure that database corruptions simply don't occur. So a database on the Mainframe is very, very safe.

- **Throughput**: Even today, it's difficult to find another platform and database management system that can process the high number of transactions that Mainframe database applications eat up for breakfast. We're talking thousands of transactions PER SECOND, each completed in less than half a second. So for larger applications the Mainframe still seems like home.

- **Security:** Correctly setup Mainframes are the most secure computing system on the planet. Period. No viruses on the Mainframe.

## The Last Word

So, we now know about Mainframes and where they sit in the computing industry. We know that:

- They're usually legacy systems holding the key data for an organization.
- They can do a lot of work, and they can do it quickly, safely and reliably.
- They're expensive, and difficult to setup and run.
- They do some things far better than any other system.
- They're hard to move from.

The fact is that the zSeries Mainframe is going to be around for many, many years to come.

# Chapter 2: What Are All These Refrigerators? Mainframe Hardware

If you walk into a computer room for the first time expecting to see this huge, magnificent Mainframe you're going to be disappointed. What you will see is a bunch of refrigerator sized boxes softly humming away. It sometimes seems that hardware manufacturers adhere to a standard refrigerator sizing scheme.

So what are all these boxes? What do they do, and why are there so many? Well, the good news is that they're not that much different from your PC - just bigger. Let's think about your PC for a second. It will have:

- One or more CPUs.
- Memory.
- Hard disks.

It will also have things like a keyboard, mouse and network adapter - but let's leave these out for a moment and concentrate on the basics.

The good news is that Mainframes also have all of this. Let's dig a bit deeper...

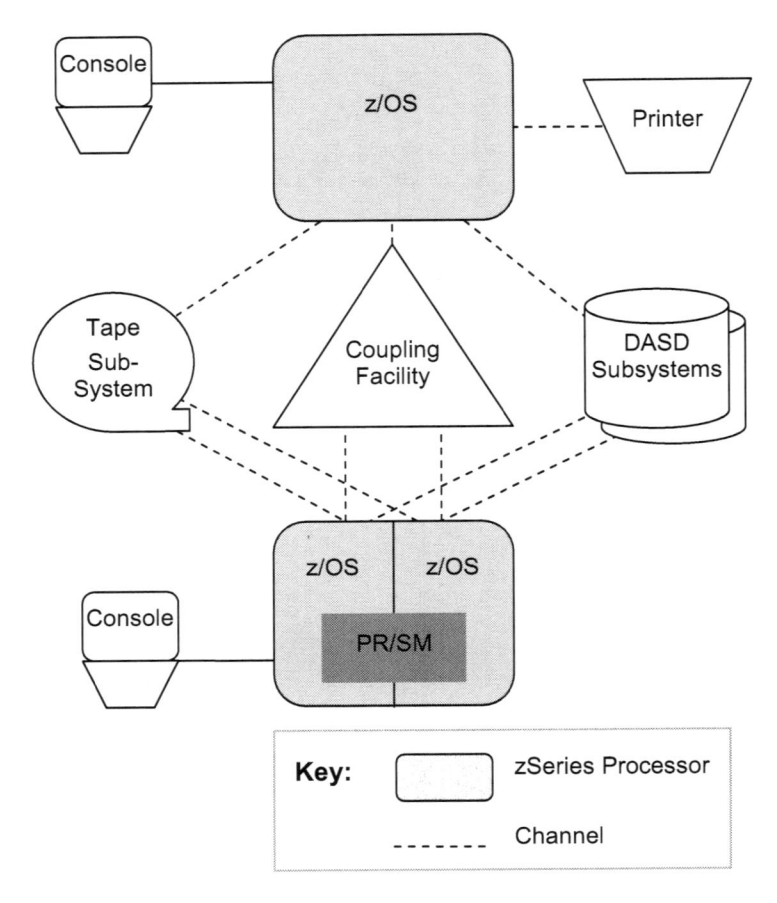

Figure 2: Mainframe Setup Example with Two Processors

# The Brains of the Organization - The Processor

The centre of it all, this is where the actual processing takes place. Holding the CPU, memory and *channels* for connecting to other hardware equipment; the processor is the first thing you think about when you think about Mainframes.

Early Mainframe processors could be huge things, needing chilled water and awkward power requirements. Today, the water cooling's gone, and processors use normal electricity outlets and take up a fraction of the space (or *footprint*). Figure 2 shows where the processor fits within a Mainframe environment and Figure 3 shows IBMs z990 zSeries processor.

**Figure 3: IBM z990 Processor** *(courtesy of IBM Archives)*

You'll also see a screen (it looks more like a PC) somewhere near the processor. This is used to control the processor. It's from this screen that you boot or start the system; called an Initial Program Load or IPL in the Mainframe world. You can also do other processor maintenance tasks here. Because it is possible to shut down the entire Mainframe from this screen it will be password protected, and be located in a very secure place.

## Who Makes Them

Only IBM.

## Sharing the Processor Around – PR/SM

The Mainframe can actually run more than one operating system *image*, thanks to IBM PR/SM™ (Processor Resource/Systems Manager™). PR/SM lets you divide one Mainframe processor into LPARs, or *logical partitions*. This is kind of like VMware®, except done by hardware. With PR/SM each LPAR can run one operating system - an operating system that thinks that it has an entire Mainframe to itself. This has a couple of advantages:

- Running multiple LPARs on the one machine can save you money in processor, maintenance, and environmental costs.

- You can *load balance*. Let's say you have two operating systems running on the machine. One is busy in the morning, the other later in the day. PR/SM can move CPU resources between LPARs from moment to moment. So you get away with a smaller processor. This saves purchase and software licensing costs.

- PR/SM can also prioritize the CPU resources. Let's say you have two LPARs, one for production, and one for testing. You can setup PR/SM so that the production LPAR gets all the processor resources it wants and the test LPAR gets what's left over.

Another way of allowing more than one operating system to run on a Mainframe is to use the z/VM operating system - something IBM calls *virtualization*. Using z/VM is exactly the same as using VMware - but z/VM has been doing this for far longer.

## *Mainframes Working Together - Parallel Sysplex and the Coupling Facility*

Larger Mainframe sites are big – very, very big. These sites simply can't run all of their work on just one operating system image or Mainframe. They need more. Multiple Mainframes also give some peace of mind as they provide redundancy (if one fails you can still do work on others).

## *Parallel Sysplex*

Over the past few years, IBM has been making it easier for Mainframes to not just communicate, but share things. These things can be anything from tape drives to databases, files, or even workloads. And they've done this with a concept called the IBM *Parallel Sysplex*®.

OK, fancy name, but it's basically just z/OS operating systems that talk and share things. You could call it *clustering*.

> ### zIIPs and zAAPs - A Helping Hand
>
> The Central Processing Unit (CPU) is the brains of any computing system, and the z/Series CPU has always been busy. One way IBM has reduced this load is to offload some of the work to other processors - either in separate boxes (like Communications Controllers and DASD Controllers), or inside the z/Series processor itself. Today the z/Series processor has two extra processors that do this - *specialty processors*:
>
> - zAAP - a CPU for Java.
> - zIIP - a CPU for database and transaction management.
>
> These specialty processors can't run z/OS itself - z/OS offloads some of the work to these processors when it can.
>
> zIIPs and zAAPs are optional - z/OS runs fine without them, and what's more they don't come free. But buying them can improve your mainframe's performance, and even reduce your software licensing costs.

## *The Coupling Facility*

The centre of the sysplex is a *coupling facility*. This is a special operating system running on either a dedicated LPAR or a separate baby zSeries Mainframe. You can't do anything else with this operating system - it just does coupling facility work.

The coupling facility is like the glue holding mainframes together. It does this by providing two things:

1. It has memory that different z/OS operating systems can share.
2. It has facilities to let z/OS operating systems share other things - a locking mechanism.

With these two features, different z/OS systems can share all sorts of things. That's all a Parallel Sysplex really is.

## Why Have a Parallel Sysplex?

So what sort of things do z/OS systems share? Let's look at a couple of examples:

### Tape Drives
Only one z/OS can use a tape drive at a time. With a Parallel Sysplex, you don't have to dedicate tape drives to individual z/OS systems. The coupling facility can control locking so any z/OS systems can use any tape drive that's free.

---

**IBM Kills The Competition with 33 Bits**

Before 2000, if you wanted a Mainframe to run operating systems like z/OS, z/VSE or z/VM, you had a choice of three manufacturers - IBM, Amdahl and Hitachi Data Systems® (HDS®).

But in 2000, IBM announced that Mainframe operating systems would be moving from the existing '31 bit' architecture to a '64 bit' architecture. There were very good reasons for doing this, but it meant that the other Mainframe manufacturers needed to spend a lot of development money to keep up. So they didn't.

This means that today all mainframe processors running z/OS are made by IBM.

---

### Workloads
Suppose you have a Parallel Sysplex with two z/OS images. It's possible to dynamically move work from one (busier) z/OS image to the other (less busy) z/OS image - without the user knowing.

### Files
If two z/OS images are going to share a file you need some way to make sure that they don't get in each other's way. z/OS has had a way of doing this for decades (using GRS, or Global Resource Sharing), but using a coupling facility and Parallel Sysplex makes it a lot faster.

But this is just the tip of the iceberg. The coupling facility can be used by any application or operating system component, for any reason you can dream up. But basically the coupling facility provides a very quick and easy way for different operating systems, and applications underneath them, to share things.

### The Second Hand Mainframe Market

IBM is the only company that makes zSeries mainframes, but they're not the only ones selling them. If your site doesn't need the very latest model, you may consider buying a refurbished, or 'second hand' mainframe from an independent dealer. These companies buy old mainframe equipment, refurbish it, and sell it again. And they usually provide support for the hardware they sell.

## *Synchronizing Your Watch – Keeping the Same Time in a Sysplex*

Like military units before an operation, every operating system in a Parallel Sysplex needs to 'synchronize their watches.' When one operating system tells another that it's done something at 10:30, that means 10:30 for all operating systems. Not 10:31 for one, and 10:29 for another. This is particularly important for things like database logs, or other time-dependant information stored in the coupling facility.

To do this all z/OS images in a Parallel Sysplex use the Server Time Protocol (STP) feature. STP is a relatively new feature – some sites may still be using an older piece of hardware called an IBM Sysplex Timer®. A Sysplex Timer is a hardware device holding a clock that individual z/OS systems connect to and use. However they are now becoming obsolete.

## Why Can't They Just Call Them Disks?

Direct Access Storage Devices (DASD) - they're just disks. Right from the beginning, IBM had disk units that were in separate boxes from the processor. They also separated out a lot of the work needed to manage these disks onto other separate boxes called *DASD controllers*. So a DASD subsystem could look like Figure 4.

Chapter 2: What Are All These Refrigerators?

```
                    to the processor
                    |           |
              ┌─────────────────────┐
              │   DASD Controller   │
              │   (3880 or 3990)    │
              └─────────────────────┘
```

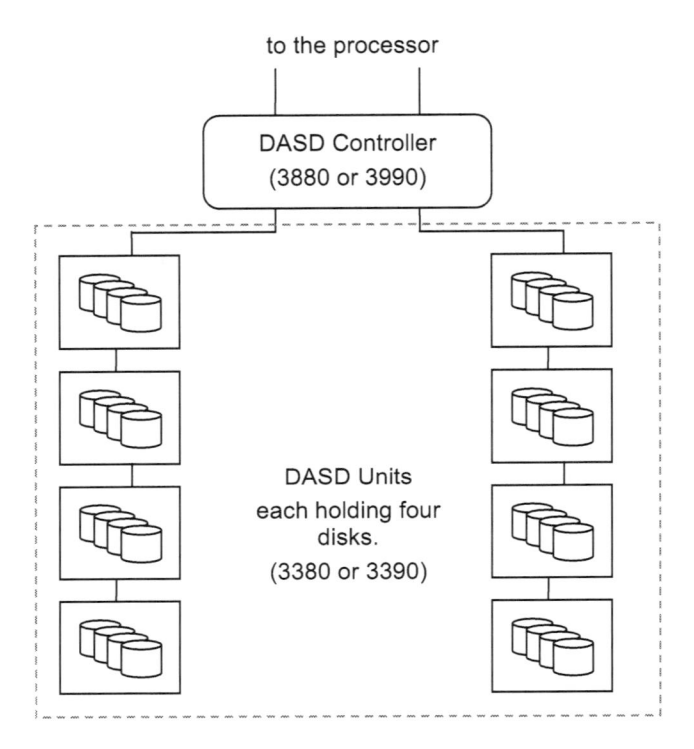

**Figure 4: Mainframe DASD String**

The DASD controller connects to the processor by more than one channel (more on these in a second), and has several DASD units 'underneath' it (all of which would be called a DASD *string*). Each DASD unit was identified by its *Volume Serial Number*.

**Figure 5: DASD Farm** *(courtesy of IBM Archives)*

What On Earth is a Mainframe?

The original controllers could only control a limited number of DASD Units so most Mainframe sites would have a lot of them. Counting all the controllers and DASD Units, there could be 20, 30, or even hundreds of these boxes (which were about twice the size of a refrigerator). So you can see how Mainframe sites required a big computer room for all this DASD. They used to be called *DASD farms,* and Figure 5 shows what they looked like.

**Figure 6: Sun StorageTek 9990V Disk Subsystem** *(courtesy of Sun StorageTek)*

## *The DASD Controller*

The DASD controllers manage disk units. More importantly, it's here that the *cache* is located. By using cache memory as a temporary storage area, the DASD controller can avoid going to the physical disk to get information. This can cut the time needed – and it can be a very big cut.

> **What's RAID?**
>
> A Redundant Array of Independent Disks (RAID) is a way of making disk hardware more reliable. It works like this:
>
> Your computer thinks it's dealing with one disk, but the disk subsystem actually spreads the contents of this 'logical' disk across several physical disks. But it doesn't just split up your data; it stores extra redundant data on all of these disks. So if one of these physical disks breaks, there's still enough information on the others to rebuild your data – and your computer is none the wiser.
>
> You can then replace the broken disk at your leisure – without any downtime.

In today's disk systems you would expect a cache read hit (the number of read operations that didn't have to go to disk) to be over 80%. Almost all disk writes are written first to cache (and control is returned to the operating system), and later written to disk by the DASD controller. This is called *DASD Fast Write*, and makes things even faster.

A big feature of Mainframe DASD (and now being used by midrange systems with Storage Area Networks) is that multiple Mainframe systems can share the same disk at the same time within a Parallel Sysplex. These multiple systems will connect to the DASD controller, which manages and queues all the requests.

## The DASD Devices

DASD devices themselves are simply disk devices. You'll hear the numbers 3380 and 3390 spoken of a lot; these are two different models of Mainframe disk devices used by Mainframes. The 3380's are older and can't store as much data as the 3390's.

## DASD Today

Today you won't find DASD controllers or DASD units in the computer room. These have been replaced by RAID disk subsystems that join together the controller and the DASD (IBM calls them an Enterprise Storage Server® or ESS) - see Figure 6 for an example. Most of these subsystems can be configured to be used by either

Mainframes or other platforms using a different connection (like SCSI - the connection used by a lot of UNIX and Windows computers).

RAID subsystems are far faster and more reliable than the older disk subsystems, however these systems still *pretend* to be the old 3380 or 3390 DASD subsystems of the past. And there are two reasons for this - the operating system expects it, and it works really, really well.

Many of these newer subsystems also offer additional goodies like disk shadowing (fast copying of one disk to another for backup or additional processing), and fast copy of data from Mainframe DASD to non-Mainframe disks on the same disk subsystem.

## *Who Makes Them*

Today, there are a couple of companies that manufacture Mainframe compatible disk subsystems, including IBM, HP, and Sun StorageTek®.

# You mean Mainframes are still using TAPE?

Your music collection may have moved from cassette tapes to CDs and MP3 players long ago, but tapes are still very important to the Mainframe world. For backups and data transportation, you just can't beat tape – it is cheap, safe, and proven.

## *Tape Subsystems for the Mainframe*

As with almost everything else, Mainframe tapes and formats are different to tapes on other platforms. The standard IBM tape types are:

**3420:** Also known as *9 track* tapes, this is a very old tape style. The tape is on a large spool (the big round thing in Figure 7) which is put into the drive. It is then wound to the empty spool on the other side of the drive. It's quite rare to see 3420 tape drives today, but there may still be some used with old applications.

> **Deciphering the IBM Hardware Code**
>
> For many years, IBM named their hardware using a four digit number. This made it very difficult for non-techies to know what they were actually referring to. And what's worse, these numbers are still used in normal conversation by Mainframe people today!
>
> So how can you decipher these? There's no guaranteed way, but as a guide look at the first 2 digits:
>
> - 33xx – Disk drives (e.g. 3380, 3390).
> - 34xx – Tape drives.
> - 35xx – Also tape drives.
> - 30xx – Processors (e.g. 3090, 3084).
> - 96xx – Also processors (e.g. 9672).
> - 43xx – Smaller processors (e.g. 4381).
> - 38xx – Printers (e.g. 3800 laser printer).
> - 32xx – Terminals or network connected printers (e.g. 3270 terminal, 3279 printer).
> - 37xx – Communications controllers (e.g. 3725, 3745).
>
> But there are always exceptions, like the 3880 (a disk controller).

**3480**: The next major step up from the 3420, the 3480 uses a cartridge about the same size as a box of 10 audio CDs (the smaller square thing in Figure 7). The amount of data you can store on each 3480 cartridge varies widely, but around 200Mbytes is a good guide.

**3490**: Using the same cartridge as the 3480, 3490s use compression to store more data. Again, the amount of data you can store varies widely, but around one GByte isn't unreasonable. The 3490E drive also uses the same cartridge, but stores the data in a more efficient method for extra storage capacity.

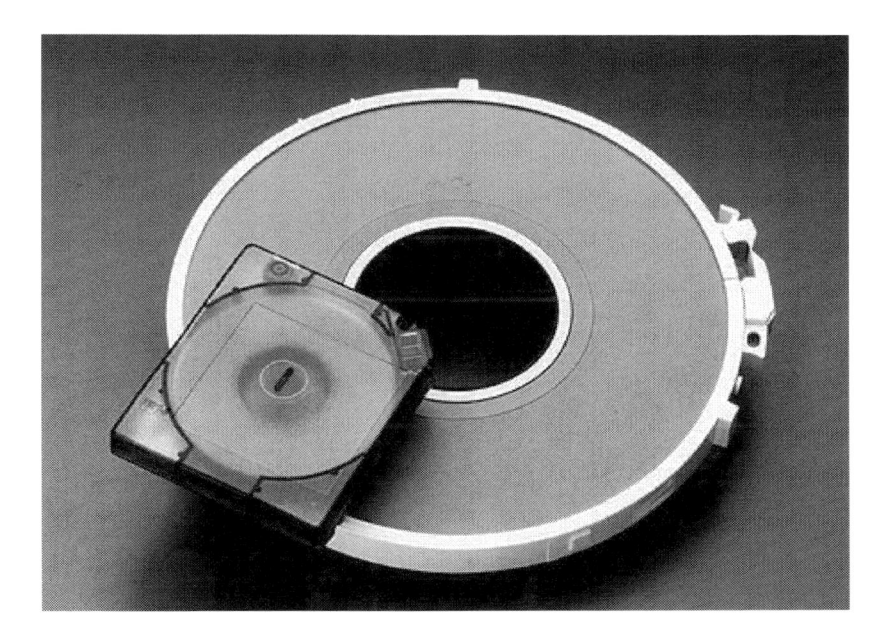

**Figure 7: 3420 (reel) and 3480 (cartridge) Tapes** *(courtesy of IBM Archives)*

**3590**: The current generation of IBM tapes. The cartridges are again the same size as a 3480, but store data differently. They can store 20+ GBytes uncompressed - more with compression.

Some other manufacturers, in particular Sun StorageTek, have produced their own tape formats that often outperform those of IBM.

## *Sharing Tape Drives between Mainframes*

Tape drives can only be used by one operating system at a time. However with z/OS, when one operating system has finished with a drive, a different one can then use it - using the benefits of a Parallel Sysplex.

## *A Library in Your Computer Room*

Let's take some time out and talk about tapes. Your Mainframe site will have a collection of these tapes - a tape library. These tapes can be divided into four groups:

- Tapes with data you want to keep.

- Tapes with data you want to keep offsite.

- Scratch tapes - tapes holding data you no longer want. These tapes are ready to be re-used, or written over.

- Tapes for transferring data in and out of your site - like tapes holding installation files for software packages.

Now, a typical Mainframe site will have a lot of these tapes - like thousands. And we need to manage these tapes - doing things like:

- Making sure we don't overwrite tapes we want to keep.

- Re-using (overwriting) tapes with data we no longer want.

- Moving tapes with data we want to keep offsite, offsite.

- Moving tapes that we no longer want offsite, back onsite.

- Keeping track when tapes enter and leave our library - like tapes used to transfer files in and out of our site.

But the work doesn't stop there. Consider:

- If we copy some data onto a tape and want to keep it for seven days. We need to keep track of the tape, and add it to our scratch tape list after that one week.

- What if a tape breaks and we lose the data on it? We may need to keep a backup of that tape.

- We should keep track of how old a tape is. So if it gets too old we can replace it with a new one (before it breaks).

So you can see that managing tapes is a lot of work. In the old days, Mainframe sites had a Tape Librarian that would do all this work by hand. Today tape management software does this for us - we talk more about this software in Chapter 7

**Figure 8: Sun StorageTek SL8500 ATL** *(courtesy of Sun StorageTek)*

## *Automated Tape Libraries*

When a program wants to read or write to a tape, the operating system tells the Mainframe Operators what tape to load, and which tape drive to load it on. So the operator goes to the tape library, gets the tape, and puts (mounts) it in the tape drive. If you have over one thousand tape mounts per day, you've got to feel sorry for the poor Operators.

But no longer! Today almost all sites don't have tape drives - they have Automated Tape Libraries (ATLs).

ATLs store the entire tape library - holding the tapes in racks. When a request to mount a certain tape (identified by its *Volume Serial Number*) is given to the ATL, a robotic system of some sort finds the tape, and automatically loads it. Operators around the world all celebrate the day when an ATL was first installed at their site.

## Tapes and Security

With z/OS security software, you can set rules for who can access which tape. However, if a tape leaves your site, this security no longer applies. For this reason, offsite tapes are held in secure places, and are checked regularly.

## Tape Compatibility

One of the big issues with tapes can be compatibility. For example, say that you backup your system to 3590 tapes and your data centre is destroyed. So you go to your Disaster Recovery site with your tapes, only to find that they have 3490 tape drives that can't read 3590 tapes. Your tapes are useless, and you're in so much trouble!

So making sure that you have compatible tapes and tape drives for your needs is very important. Most tape drives can read older formats (e.g. a 3590E drive will read a 3590 tape) providing you are using the same tape cartridge type. Also, some manufacturers let you write out in older format for compatibility (e.g. The Sun StorageTek 9940 drives can write to tapes in 3490E and 3590 formats).

## Who Makes Them

The main manufacturers are IBM and Sun StorageTek.

# Other Removable Media

Although you can get CD drives for Mainframes, they aren't popular - and most Mainframes don't even have a CD drive. You can manage CDs using similar software as for tapes (or in some cases, exactly the same software).

## Who Makes Them
Mainly IBM.

# Printers

They may have talked about the 'paperless office' in the past, but today, everyone still wants to print. And printing in Mainframe terms can be a LOT of printing – bank statements, reports, form letters, and advertising material. Let's look at the two categories of Mainframe printers:

## Printers on the Network

Before the Personal Computer revolution, if you wanted to print, you would use a printer that talked to the Mainframe using the SNA Mainframe network protocol. There would usually be some printing software that would manage the printers, and Mainframe applications would have to have a facility to let the user print.

Today, these types of systems are rare, as organizations use Local Area Network printers for most small scale printing. Mainframes can also be setup to connect and print directly to these Local Area Network printers.

## Enterprise Printers

By Enterprise, we mean the big printers that connect straight to the Mainframe via channels (more on these in a moment). These are the printers that can print account statements for 10,000 of the bank's customers in an hour, or bills for 15,000 customers of a telephone company.

Enterprise printers usually use IBM's Advanced Function Printing (AFP) software (yes, you need special IBM software to run these - and it doesn't come for free) and handle large scale work. Today, these printers can also be offline, meaning they're not connected to the Mainframe. Rather, they are connected over a network or use tape cartridges.

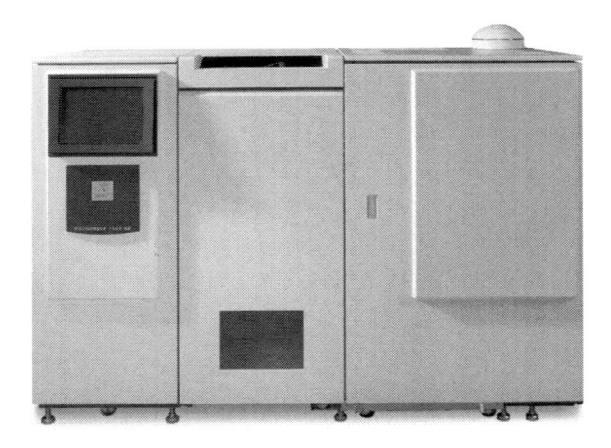

Figure 9: Xerox DocuPrint 525 Enterprise Printer *(courtesy of Xerox)*

## *Who Makes Them?*
Mainly InfoPrint™ and Xerox®.

# Connecting the Boxes – Channels

It's all very nice having these boxes sitting quietly in your data centre. But they all need to be connected – to talk to each other. Mainframe people call these connections *channels*, and there are three main types:

### Parallel Channel
These channels have almost been phased out. The oldest of the channels, they use a pair of very, very thick copper cables called *Bus and Tag* cables. They can only be used over distances up to 122m (400 feet), and have a top transfer speed of 4.5 Mbytes per second. Each parallel channel can only be used by one z/OS image.

### ESCON
IBM ESCON® replaced the copper cable pairs with a single thin fiber optic cable – and Mainframe hardware engineers worldwide no longer needed strong arms. They can be used for distances up to 3km (1.87 miles), and have a top data transfer rate of 17 Mbytes per second.

ESCON channels can also be shared by z/OS images running on the same physical machine.

Figure 10: Parallel Channel Cable *(courtesy Patrick Finnegan and www.computer-refuge.org)*

**FICON**
The new kid on the block, IBM FICON® is also a single fiber optic cable that looks deceptively like an ESCON cable. There are a few different types:

- **FICON FCV – FICON Conversion mode:** This is where it 'pretends' to be an ESCON channel, so it can be used to connect to a system via its ESCON port.

- **FICON Native**: Data rates in the range of 100 Mbytes per second, and distances of around 9km.

- **FICON FCP**: (FICON Channel Protocol) This is where the Mainframes can now access Storage Area Networks using FCP switches. This is also the protocol that lets the Linux operating system running on the Mainframe to access SCSI devices. You can get speeds of in excess of 200 Mbytes per second, and distances of around 20km.

# What Are Environmentals?

When Mainframe managers talk about environmentals, they're talking about two things: the computer room and electricity.

## *The Computer Room*

Your Mainframe needs a computer room. This will be a room that has:

- Air conditioning to keep the temperature constant.
- Constant humidity.
- Usually a raised floor – leaving a gap between where you're standing and the real floor. This allows space for cables to run underneath.

The chances are that your Operators will work in this room (we talk about Operators in Chapter 8), and because your Mainframe's important, this room will be in a very secure place.

## *Electricity*

No electricity, no Mainframe - there's no surprise here. So your computer room needs a reliable electricity supply – and this means an Uninterruptible Power Supply, or UPS. The UPS sits between the electricity supply and your computer room, and is designed to give you a short amount of time (usually 10-30 minutes) of electricity if the electricity supply fails. So you're protected from short blackouts (no electricity) and brownouts (a very short failure – for example a half second).

Now, you're already thinking "what if the power failure is longer than what the UPS can cover?" Mainframe sites have already thought of this, and will usually have a backup generator. So the UPS covers the time between a power failure and the generator starting.

> ### Doing it Better Than IBM – Gene Amdahl
>
> When you think of the original genius who can build a computer from an electric toothbrush and a couple of batteries, then you're thinking of someone like computing pioneer Gene Amdahl.
>
> Armed with a degree in engineering and a doctorate in theoretical physics, he worked on many early IBM computers from 1952 to 1955. In 1960, he was one of the main architects of the IBM System/360– the precursor to the current Mainframe today.
>
> When IBM rejected his development ideas in 1970, he decided to make his own Mainframes. In 1975, his company Amdahl, shipped its first IBM 'compatible.' This computer was compatible with the IBM System 370/165, but it was faster and cheaper.
>
> He stayed with Amdahl for nine years before moving on. Amdahl however, continued building IBM compatible Mainframes under the Fujitsu umbrella until 2000.
>
> Pure computing scientists know Gene Amdahl for his 'Amdahl's Law' – a formula for estimating the maximum expected improvement to an entire computing system when only a part of it's improved.

# The Last Word

So, we now know about the major building blocks, or hardware pieces that make up a typical Mainframe. There are some more pieces of hardware we haven't gone into yet, in particular the Communications hardware, but that'll come later.

We know that a Mainframe generally has a processor, coupling facility, disk subsystem, tape subsystem, and possibly some printers. These are usually all connected by either ESCON or FICON channels.

Mainframes also need a computer room with a regular and reliable electricity supply.

# Chapter 3: The z/OS Jigsaw Puzzle - The Many Pieces of z/OS

z/OS is far and away the most popular operating system for Mainframes. And although it doesn't get a lot of attention, it's the structure on which all your Mainframe operations rely. If z/OS doesn't work, nothing will. For decades major organizations have relied on z/OS to keep their Mainframes running – and z/OS has delivered.

So it should be easy… you buy an operating system, and it works, providing everything you need. However in the 1970s IBM broke the z/OS operating system into different parts. This means that today, your software maintenance bill can reach from your floor to the ceiling. But it's also allowed third party (non-IBM) vendors to compete with IBM for your organization's software budget.

So let's look at all the pieces of z/OS…

## What You Get When You Buy z/OS

- The z/OS operating system.
- Two ways to talk to people and other computers: SNA and TCP/IP.
- A way to access and manage files: DFSMSdfp™.
- A second operating system at no extra cost: UNIX (USS or UNIX System Services).

### The James Bond of Operating Systems – The Many Names of z/OS

Like a secret agent, z/OS has had many names over the years:

- OS/VS2 MVS in 1972. Based on the older OS/360 operating system.
- MVS/SP™ in 1979.
- MVS/XA™ in 1981. The XA stands for Extended Architecture. MVS/XA went from a '24-bit' to '31-bit' architecture, making it able to handle lots more memory.
- MVS/ESA™ in 1988.
- OS/390 in 1997.
- z/OS in 2000. z/OS moved to a 64-bit architecture, making it able to handle even more memory.

To make things more confusing there's also z/OSe. z/OS at a bargain price, it can't run legacy applications (no IMS® or COBOL) – only newer technology like C++, Java, Websphere® and DB2®. However you won't see z/OSe around for long as IBM replaces it with normal z/OS with a different (and cheaper) license - System z New Application License Charge (zNALC).

- A way to use z/OS interactively (i.e. from a terminal): TSO/E and ISPF.
- A Job Entry Subsystem: JES2 or JES3 (your choice).
- Runtime environments for languages: IBM Language Environment®.
- A way to manage workloads - Workload Manager (WLM).
- A way to bind programs so they are ready for execution - the Binder. More about this in Chapter 6.
- A way to install software on your Mainframe: SMP/E.
- A utility to keep track of hardware and software errors: EREP.
- High Level Assembler (HLASM) – an Assembler programming language.
- An HTTP Server – so you can host web pages.

- And a few other utilities to do things like format disks.

### What is an Operating System?

It's software that every computer has. It makes your life easier by doing things like:

- Acting as a 'middle man' between you and the hardware. To see something on the screen, enter something using a keyboard or mouse, or write something to disk; there's a whole lot of work that needs to be done.

- Managing security.

- Helping you use a network.

- Allowing many different things to run at the same time without getting in each other's way (*multiprocessing*).

- Handling problems. If something goes wrong, the operating system should clean up everything, and let work continue.

- Providing utilities to make your life easier, like:
    o View, create and delete files.
    o See what tasks are running on the system.
    o Determine what problems are happening, and fix them.
    o See who's been doing what and when (an audit facility).

Take Microsoft Windows – it does all the 'extra' work needed when you:

- Start your computer - checking all the hardware.
- Play a CD.
- Use a network (including talking to the network card).
- Do anything with files (using Microsoft® Windows® Explorer).
- Show you the nice screen with Windows and pictures.
- Move the pointer on the screen when you move your mouse.
- Start an application like Microsoft Word.
- Administer things using the Control Panel
- Run more than one program at the same time.

Chapter 3: The z/OS Jigsaw Puzzle                                    45

This sounds good doesn't it? Everything you need to get your system running. Now, there are only twelve things you really need to know about z/OS.

# 12 Things You Need To Know About z/OS

## 1. z/OS Runs Lots of Things at the Same Time

When z/OS was being first developed, computers were very, very expensive. So everyone had to share them. This means that z/OS has been designed to run work for lots of different people at the same time.

Think of an exclusive restaurant with individual booths. When you sit down, the waiter pulls a curtain, and you can't see anyone else. You could be forgiven for thinking that you've got the whole restaurant to yourself – your own waiter, chefs, everything. But behind that curtain the waiter is serving others, and everyone's sharing the resources of the chefs in the kitchen. z/OS is very much like that.

Every task running in z/OS runs in an *address space* - its very own booth. Each address space thinks it's the only one running on the Mainframe - and that it has the entire computer to itself. But behind the curtain z/OS is sharing the resources (memory, CPU, I/O) between all the address spaces – and there can be hundreds of them. Address spaces are like *processes* in UNIX and Windows.

## 2. z/OS Handles Large Workloads

This may sound obvious but let's think about this for a moment. From the beginning z/OS has been designed to handle workloads that often exceed what the computer can handle. So z/OS has needed to be able to prioritize work: the most important first, the less important following. So in order, a good priority system would be:

1. Systems Tasks.

2. Production online.
3. Production batch.
4. Other work if there's time.

What the priorities are in your organization depends on what you want. z/OS allows your Systems Programmer to specify in a lot of detail what should be done first and what can wait, using a free z/OS feature called Workload Manager (WLM). What's more, z/OS is designed to run the computer's CPU at 100%. That's right, if your Mainframe is running at 100% CPU capacity, don't panic – things could be running perfectly.

## 3. It's Hard to Crash z/OS

You need your Mainframe to just keep running –you don't want an error in one application program crashing the whole system. z/OS knows this and separates these address spaces very well. It's impossible for a normal program to affect another address space – like crash it, or change its memory. Not unless you make it a system task.

z/OS is also king at cleaning up after problems. Early programs running on Mainframes used to crash all the time. IBM has spent a lot of time making z/OS robust, so these crashes don't interfere with other work. Just as importantly everything is cleaned up after a crash, and other tasks aren't affected.

z/OS includes something called Environmental Record Editing and Printing (EREP). EREP records every software and hardware error. Your operations staff will check this record daily.

## 4. z/OS Is Efficient

In the early days of z/OS, there were never enough resources - memory, CPU and I/O. So IBM in developing z/OS has done a lot of work to make it efficient, so more work can run on less. Look at the three main processor resources:

**CPU**: z/OS manages who gets to use the CPU, and for how long. We've already talked about prioritization and how Systems Programmers can determine which tasks are more important.

**Memory**: Mainframes often only have as much memory as your PC. z/OS doesn't need any more because it is so efficient.

**I/O**: You've only got a certain number of channels leaving your Mainframe. If these fill up with work (which used to happen quite a lot in the early days of z/OS) then you're going to have to wait. z/OS tries to avoid doing I/O altogether by *buffering* records in memory. Let's say you need a record from a file, so you go and read it. The chances are that z/OS will also read a couple more records into memory. So if you decide you want the next record it's already in memory waiting for you.

## 5. z/OS Has the Best Recording

z/OS comes with its own personal scribe - System Management Facilities (SMF). SMF is used to record information about how z/OS is running - and it's very efficient. You can record a lot of things without impacting z/OS performance. z/OS uses SMF to record things like:

- When a file is opened or deleted (who did it).
- When the system is booted up (IPLed).
- When something is started (like a batch job).
- Performance information when a batch job finishes (how long it took and how much CPU, memory and I/O it used).

Anyone can use SMF facilities – including security software (for audit), performance monitoring software, and Transaction and Database Managers (we talk about these a bit later).

Using SMF, z/OS has the most extensive recording of any operating system –it's used for things like:

- Security audits.

- Performance monitoring – finding any performance related problems.
- Capacity planning – is the Mainframe big enough?
- Resource accounting – who's using what resource, and how much should we charge them?

You'll be saving many of your SMF records for years, but these records are only useful if you can get information from them. For that, you need *decision support* software. We talk more about this software in the Accessorize chapter.

---

**Online and Batch**

When IBM started designing the operating system that was to become z/OS, it was designed for batch – doing a whole lot of tasks or transactions in one go. An example of a batch task today would be calculating interest for every bank account, or printing all the bank statements. Batch tasks can be quick, or can run for hours. Today, running complex batch streams is one of the strengths of z/OS.

Online work is when there's a human at a computer that has hit a key and is expecting something to happen. This came to z/OS a little later than batch. An example of an online transaction is when you use an Automated Teller Machine (ATM).

In fact a way to login to z/OS from a terminal and do things like edit files only came to Mainframes via a separate product: Time Sharing Option (TSO). TSO (or TSO/E as it's now called) now comes with z/OS.

---

## 6. You Need a Job Entry Subsystem

z/OS has always been designed to run batch *jobs* – tasks that do a lot of work without someone at a computer controlling it. Every Mainframe site will have things that need to run in batch.

To run batch on z/OS, you need a Job Entry Subsystem – this is software that:

- Accepts batch jobs submitted – translates the control statements into machine-readable form, and queues them ready for processing.

- Creates and controls address spaces in which the batch jobs will run – *initiators*.
- If the batch job is to run on a different machine, sends it to that machine.
- Gives the batch jobs to z/OS to run when they're ready.
- Allocates and frees any files that the batch job needs.
- Saves all job output in *spool* – an area on a disk especially used for job input and output. Output can be job messages showing whether it's been successful or not, or it could be reports to be printed or sent.
- Lets Operators and users control their jobs and the output they create.

When you want to submit a batch job, you need to tell the JES some things:

- Where the job will run – on which system.
- If the job will actually run, or if you want it *held* (waiting for someone to come along later and *release* the job).
- Which programs to run – you can actually run more than one program – in different job *steps*.
- Where to find the actual programs - in what file.
- What files need to be created – including how big to make them, what type they must be, and where they should go.
- What files need to be read, written or deleted.
- Where any output should be sent.
- Which userid to use.
- Where to bill the resources used by the batch job.

You don't think of these issues with most other operating systems, but z/OS is special.

You tell z/OS all these things using a language called the Job Control Language (JCL). This language is actually quite detailed, and gives you a lot of control over your job. For example, you can tell the JES that if the first part (or *step*) of the job fails, it must not run any other steps.

IBM gives you two choices for your JES: JES2 and JES3. JES2 is by far the most common.

## 7. z/OS Files are Weird

You know about files – they hold your data, and you can read it with an application like Windows Notepad. How different can z/OS files be? Very! For a start, they have a different name: *datasets*.

z/OS files are effectively mini-databases. Every file is made up of records. When you create (or *allocate*) a file, you have to tell z/OS how long each record will be (or the maximum length, if you want variable length records). You'll also tell z/OS:

**Volume Serial Number**: This is the name of the disk or disks to put the dataset on (a dataset can be on more than one disk).

**How Big:** Datasets look like one file, but they're really broken into chunks or *extents*. You tell z/OS how big to make the primary extent (the first one), and any secondary extents (the rest). When you use the dataset, you use the primary extent until it fills up, then z/OS finds other extents for you to use.

**Blocksize** – z/OS uses a *blocking* file system. When it goes to disk to get some information, it will get one block (which is usually more than one record). You tell z/OS how big a block you want to use for each dataset (though there are rules). Setting a good blocksize can make a big difference to your performance.

**Dataset Type** – z/OS has a few different dataset types:

- Sequential – a 'flat file,' very similar to your normal UNIX or Windows files.

- Partitioned Dataset (PDS) – this is a dataset made up of sequential datasets – kind of like a directory in UNIX or a folder in Windows. Because of their structure, PDSs often have to be *compressed* to reclaim old space that is no longer used.

- A newer type of PDS is called a PDSE (PDS Extended) – this doesn't have to be compressed, and can be faster than PDSs.

- Basic Direct Access Method (BDAM): This means that applications accessing this dataset are using their own 'access method' – not one supplied by IBM.

- Variable Sequential Access Method (VSAM): A database in a dataset. This is such an efficient way of storing data that IMS and DB2 use it for their databases.

- Hierarchical File System (HFS): This is a dataset that is used by z/OS UNIX to store UNIX file systems. zFS is a newer version of HFS and does the same thing but a little better. z/OS UNIX thinks these files are actually disks.

### ASCII and EBCDIC

Computers store information as numbers. They convert every character (letter, digit, and symbol) to a number that they can store. Almost every computer you'll find uses ASCII (American Standard Code for Information Interchange) – a standard way of doing this conversion. Using ASCII the character 'a' is stored as 97, and 'L' as 76.

The zSeries Mainframe is different. It uses EBCDIC (Extended Binary Coded Decimal Interchange Code). So the character 'a' is stored as 129 and 'L' as 211.

This means that when Mainframe applications to talk with the outside world, they need to do a lot of translations between EBCDIC and ASCII.

z/OS today makes the effort of allocating a dataset easier by including a free feature called DFSMS™ (Data Facility Systems Managed Storage). Using DFSMS, your Systems Programmer can setup defaults to save you the effort of deciding all these options – and even override your choices with ones that are better.

## 8. You Can't Logon to z/OS

It seems weird, but z/OS itself doesn't have a way for you to logon and control it, and we've talked earlier how you actually logon to an application called TSO/E (Time Sharing Option Extended) to manage z/OS. TSO/E gives you an interface that's similar to the old Microsoft MS-DOS® prompt, so it's pretty hard to use. That's why z/OS also comes with ISPF (Interactive System Productivity Facility) that runs under TSO/E. This give you a much nicer way of doing things – using full screens (or *panels*) and providing standard utilities to do things like editing datasets.

TSO and ISPF were originally used to manage z/OS – edit datasets, control jobs, look at error messages and output. But like many things with z/OS, IBM has continued to provide more and more facilities. So today you often see smaller applications running under TSO/E.

## 9. You Get UNIX with z/OS

We mentioned before that z/OS also comes with UNIX, but we lied a bit. Technically z/OS comes with a POSIX® compliant UNIX shell called UNIX Systems Services (USS). But to anyone using z/OS, it's UNIX. Being POSIX compliant means that it follows all the standard rules needed to be called UNIX. This gives z/OS users two big benefits:

- UNIX applications written in languages like C, C++ and Java™ can now run on USS. This means that programmers with these skills can write Mainframe applications - without the z/OS knowledge that traditional Mainframe programmers need. They can also copy existing applications from other UNIX platforms.

- The Mainframe can now talk to the internet. You can everything do anything from hosting web pages on the Mainframe to web enabling legacy applications.

USS also gives users an alternative way to logon to z/OS if they don't want to use TSO/E.

## 10. z/OS Has a Console

Your Mainframe will have an operations room, where you'll have Operators doing all sorts of things (we'll talk about Operators more in Chapter 8). But you can bet that at the heart of the operations room is the z/OS console.

These consoles are like a constant news feed – letting Operators know what's going on, what problems are happening, and anything else they need to know. Operators can also enter z/OS commands through this console – no need to logon.

You can have lots of these consoles – some you can use through TSO/E or other software. But you'll have just one master console per z/OS – and the master doesn't need a network, it just plugs straight into the Mainframe. So even if there's a problem with the network, you can still see what's happening.

> **What is a Started Task?**
>
> It's a system task. It looks similar to a batch job, but is started and stopped by the z/OS Operator (or Automated Operations software). Anything that works with the system, and needs to be up and running all the time is usually a started task. For example, Transaction and Database managers run as one or more started tasks.
>
> You sometimes see 'Started Task' written in shorthand as STC (for Started Task Control).

## 11. If You Don't Like z/OS – Change It

z/OS (and lots of other Mainframe software like CICS, IMS and RACF) lets you change things you don't like, or add extra things you want. The way you do this is to write small mini-programs called *exits* – usually done by your Systems Programmer.

Let's take an example. z/OS gives you an exit called IEFUJI. This exit gets control whenever someone submits a batch job – and it can tell your JES know whether it should let this job run or not. If you don't code anything here, JES just takes the job and processes it. You could write some code that does things like reject the job if:

- The job name is wrong (doesn't conform to your standards).
- If the person submitting the job doesn't have some security privileges or isn't allowed to submit jobs at that time of day.

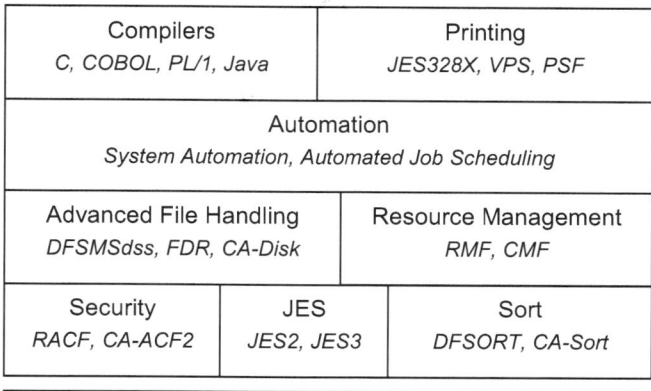

| Compilers | Printing |
|---|---|
| C, COBOL, PL/1, Java | JES328X, VPS, PSF |

| Automation |
|---|
| System Automation, Automated Job Scheduling |

| Advanced File Handling | Resource Management |
|---|---|
| DFSMSdss, FDR, CA-Disk | RMF, CMF |

| Security | JES | Sort |
|---|---|---|
| RACF, CA-ACF2 | JES2, JES3 | DFSORT, CA-Sort |

| Runtime | Communications | Logon |
|---|---|---|
| LE | SNA, TCP/IP | TSO/E, ISPF |

| Workloads | Format Disks | Basic File Handling |
|---|---|---|
| WLM | ICKDSF | DFSMS, DFSMSdfp |

| Other Utilities | Recording | UNIX |
|---|---|---|
|  | SMF | USS |

| Web Hosting | Error Recording | Assembler |
|---|---|---|
| HTTP Server | EREP | HLASM |

Base z/OS Functions

z/OS

Figure 11: Operating System Functions Inside and Outside of z/OS

## 12. z/OS Isn't Enough

This covers the things you do get with z/OS, and you can see this summarized in Figure 11. With all of this you can certainly setup a very basic operating system, but you won't be able to do much. There are more things you need to buy.

# What You Don't Get When You Buy z/OS

z/OS is only the basic operating system. It doesn't give you:

- Security Software.
- A way to manage an archive datasets.
- Sorting Software.
- Software to measure resource usage and performance.
- A way to automatically manage your system, network and batch.
- A way to print.
- Compilers for application programming languages.

Let's look at these a bit more closely.

## Security Software

OK, technically you can run z/OS without some external security software, but no-one does. z/OS just doesn't provide enough security facilities. So everyone buys some security software.

The three main choices are:

- RACF – IBM's Resource Access Control Facility, part of IBM z/OS Security Server.
- CA-ACF2®.
- CA-TopSecret®.

All of these have a database for storing userids and rules. Rules specify whether someone has access to:

- Read, write, create or delete datasets or databases.
- Run programs.
- Logon to Transaction Managers like CICS or IMS.
- Submit batch jobs.
- Look at output from batch jobs.
- Issue z/OS System Commands.

---

### The Mainframe Secret Code - Acronyms

IBM loves acronyms (just look at the name). It seems that IBM has thousands of acronyms for just about everything. So you'd think that learning what all these acronyms actually stand for would help understand what they mean. Great idea, but wrong. Have a look at some examples:

**TSO – Time Sharing Option**: TSO is a way of using a terminal to maintain z/OS.

**SPOOL – Simultaneous Peripheral Offload On Line**: JES2 uses SPOOL to store jobs coming in, and output going out.

**DASD – Direct Access Storage Device**: Disk.

**MVS – Multiple Virtual System:** An operating system.

**CICS – Customer Information Control System**: A Transaction Manager.

What these acronyms stand for really doesn't help at all does it? So most Mainframe users just use the acronym, and don't worry too much about what it stands for. IBM has a good website where you can find common IBM terms and acronyms: http://www.ibm.com/ibm/terminology

---

All three software packages also have:

- Utilities to backup and restore the databases holding the userids and rules.
- A way to record security information to SMF for audit purposes.

Chapter 3: The z/OS Jigsaw Puzzle

- A way for a Security Administrator to make changes to userids and rules.

## Managing and Archiving Datasets

A Mainframe site will have lots of datasets – like thousands, or even tens (or hundreds) of thousands. z/OS comes with ways of managing these datasets (deleting, renaming, moving, backing up, restoring) – but these aren't great. Here are some reasons why:

- You need to use different utilities to copy different types of dataset. For example, IEBGENER to copy a sequential dataset, IEBCOPY to copy a PDS, and IDCAMS to copy a VSAM dataset.

- These utilities are fine for single datasets – but you have to specifically name every individual dataset. When you want to process 800 datasets, these utilities start to lose their appeal.

- These utilities can't backup an entire disk.

So you'll have software that can manage the lot. The three main options are IBM DFSMSdss™ (Data Support Services), CA Disk™ Backup and Restore, and Innovation® FDR™.

It doesn't stop there. Most sites will want some way to 'archive' their datasets. This means that datasets that haven't been used for a period of time are stored on compressed disk or tape. Products like IBM's DFSMShsm™ (Hierarchical Storage Manager) or Innovation ABR™ help with this. They archive unused datasets automatically, and bring them back automatically when someone wants to use them.

## Sorting Software

Commercial data processing needs to sort stuff. Lots of stuff. Often. With small amounts of data this isn't a problem, you can write a quick little program to do this. But when you need to sort hundreds of thousands (or millions) of records fast – that little program you wrote isn't good enough.

You'll need sorting software. Some of the options include:

- IBM DFSORT™.
- CA-SORT™.
- SyncSort™.

These sorting programs are actually very smart and can:

- Look at the data to be sorted, and pick the best sorting algorithm to use.
- Merge multiple files into one.
- Create output ready for reporting.
- Be called from within an application program.
- Use datasets for sorting if there's too much data to sort in memory.

But perhaps most importantly, large organizations need to be as efficient as possible when sorting. So these sorting packages sort using the minimum of computing resources (CPU, memory and I/O).

## *Resource Measurement*

We talked earlier about SMF and how it can be used for performance monitoring, resource accounting and capacity planning. However SMF doesn't produce these records itself. You need software like:

- IBM RMF™ (Resource Monitoring Facility).
- BMC CMF MONITOR™.

This software monitors all work on the Mainframe. It looks at resource usage (CPU, memory and I/O), and can also look for bottlenecks and other performance problems.

## *Automation*

Mainframes can be complicated things to run. In the past, you'd have teams of Operators looking after your Mainframe 24 hours a day, seven days a week. We talk more about what an Operator does in Chapter 8, but you don't need so many of them today – not if you've got automation software doing some of their work.

There are two main types of automation software, Systems Automation and Automated Job Scheduling.

---

### A Program to Install Programs - SMP/E

z/OS includes free a program called SMP/E (Systems Management Program / Extended). Almost all software and software fixes for the Mainframe are 'packaged' so that they can be installed using SMP/E (including z/OS and SMP/E itself!). Here's how it works:

You setup SMP/E on your mainframe with some options, including where the software is to be installed (the dataset names).

- You tell SMP/E to *receive* the software or fix. It loads the software (usually from one or more tapes) that is in a special SMP/E format onto the Mainframe and checks it.

- You tell SMP/E to *apply* the software. SMP/E first checks that any *pre-requisites* (software or fixes that must be already installed) are installed (or has been received), and copies the software to the datasets you specified earlier. It will also bind load modules and remove any modules that it replaces (like an older version).

And Voila! Your software is ready to be customized and run. So the idea is that the software modules are only changed through SMP/E. It can record what changes have been made and manages prerequisites. But it goes a bit further.

SMP/E will stop you from installing a fix if you've already installed a *superseding* fix (a later one that replaces it). It also helps you keep track of what software (and versions) has been installed, what modules belong to which software, and which fixes have already been installed.

After applying software, you can *accept* the software. This gives you a 'clean point' - a copy of the software that you know works. So if a later install causes problems, you can undo it.

---

What On Earth is a Mainframe?

## Systems Automation

This automates things you need to do to start, run and stop a z/OS system. So you can do things like:

- Automatically do things whenever z/OS starts up or shuts down.
- Automatically issue z/OS commands (like starting and stopping things) at certain times of the day.
- Automatically do things when specific events happen (like submitting a job when a dataset fills up).
- Monitor the z/OS console and let the Operator know if there's a problem.

This all sounds simple, but with so many things happening and running on every z/OS, it quickly gets complicated. Systems automation products include:

- IBM Tivoli Systems Automation.
- CA-Ops/MVS®.
- BMC MAINVIEW AUTOOPERATOR™.
- ASG-Zack™.

## Automated Job Scheduling

Imagine you have a batch schedule of 150 jobs running every night:

- Five jobs need files sent from external computer systems
- Most jobs can't run until another batch job has run successfully.
- Three jobs only run on Fridays.
- Two jobs only run on the last day of the month.
- Six jobs have to wait for CICS to be shutdown.
- Three jobs need special (and different) paper to be loaded in your enterprise printer.

You can see that managing all these jobs can get very complicated. Job scheduling software helps you out here. It can:

- Check that jobs complete OK
- Stop jobs from running if a previous job has failed.
- Wait for a file to be created before starting a job.

Some automated job schedulers include:

- BMC CONTROL-M/ENTERPRISE MANAGER™.
- IBM Tivoli Workload Scheduler (TWS).
- CA-7®.
- ASG-Zeke™.

## *Printing from z/OS*

It seems amazing but z/OS doesn't have a way to print. Most small print jobs today are done on Local Area Networked (LAN) printers. However you may have some older printers, or very large print jobs like a bank's monthly account statements.

Older networked printers used to connect to z/OS over a Mainframe network. To print to these you would send your output to a JES output queue, and then use software like IBM JES328X, or Levi, Ray & Shoup VPS® (Virtual Printer Support) to take this output and send it to the printer.

IBM has also produced a standard way of printing to larger printers from the Mainframe – Advanced Function Presentation (AFP). But to use this you'll need the IBM Print Services Facility™ (PSF) software. This takes the output from the JES output queue, formats it for AFP, and sends it to the printer.

## *z/OS Compilers*

Your application programs may be written in a language such as C, COBOL or Java. However these programs need to be compiled – and the compilers don't come with z/OS (they're extra). We talk more about compilers in Chapter 6.

> ### What Else Can Run on a Mainframe?
>
> Although most z/Series Mainframes run z/OS, there are several other IBM operating systems that can also run on them:
>
> **z/TPF –Transaction Processing Facility**: z/TPF is all about transaction management – lots of transactions being handled very, very fast. Its main use is for airline reservation systems, but it's also used by hotel reservation systems, credit card transaction processing, and even the emergency 911 system for the New York Police Force. Many z/TPF sites use z/OS for batch processing.
>
> **z/VSE**™: The little brother of z/OS, it used to be called DOS/VSE®. When the OS/360 operating system (which later became z/OS) was developed in the 1960s for the then new System/360 machines, IBM found out that this operating system was too big for the smaller System/360 models (oops!). Their solution – another operating system: DOS/360. IBM figured that this would cover this 'hole' for a few years, then everyone would move up. IBM was wrong.
>
> Today, z/VSE is still around and actively supported by IBM.
>
> **z/VM**®: An operating system in its own right that can run applications, z/VM is perhaps more often used as a 'hosting' operating system. This means that lots of other mainframe operating systems can run as 'guests' of z/VM simultaneously - similar to PR/SM or VMware. z/VM has seen a resurgence with the hosting of z/Linux operating systems on the mainframes.
>
> **z/Linux** – Linus Torvald's UNIX now runs natively on IBM z/Series mainframes. With z/VM allowing up to 255 operating systems running on the one Mainframe, this can be an attractive alternative for sites with large numbers of UNIX machines.

# The Last Word

So you can see that there's a lot that makes up z/OS – and even more that you need to buy before you've got something useful. The bad news is that all this just gives you the base, or structure. Without databases and applications to access them, you're not doing any real work yet.

# Chapter 4: Talking to z/OS - Networks and Communications

You don't have to be in the same room as the Mainframe to use it. So you do need a way to talk to the Mainframe - a Mainframe network.

z/OS comes with z/OS Communication Server. This gives you two different networking options: SNA and TCP/IP.

## SNA Networks

Systems Network Architecture (SNA) networks are the original Mainframe networks. But to talk about SNA we need a bit of a history lesson. So let's see how SNA networks *used* to be.

### *The 3270 Terminal – Your Window to the Mainframe*

To talk to a Mainframe, the chances are that you'd use a 3270 terminal. Well, more like a 3270 'style' terminal - IBM and other companies made quite a few different ones. The 3270 was different from terminals used by other computer systems. Amongst other things it had a slightly different keyboard, including an extra Enter key in the bottom right hand corner (see the black key in Figure 12).

So what does this mean? With most terminals, when you hit any key you talk to the computer. The 3270 was different – it was connected to a box called *a Cluster Controller* (there were two main models: the 3174 and the newer 3274), that in turn talked to the Mainframe. This meant that the Mainframe only saw what you had entered after you hit that extra Enter key, saving it from having to look after each individual terminal. And when you have thousands of terminals, this is a big saving.

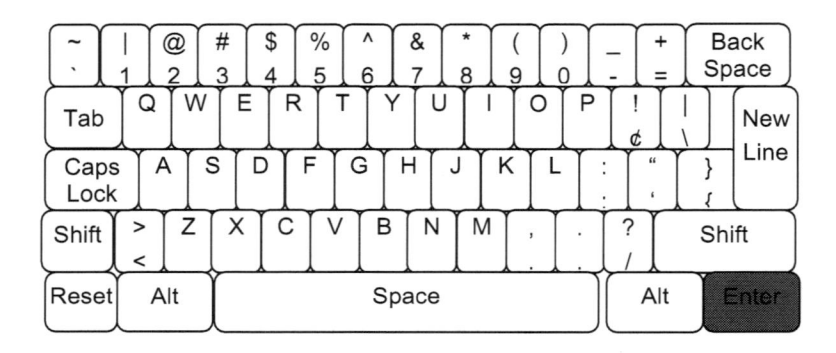

**Figure 12: A 3270 Style Keyboard**

(We've actually lied to you a bit here. The 3270 keyboard also had some other special keys - what they did depended on the application. These keys would also send data right back to the Mainframe. But let's just stick to the basics).

So, because of this most applications running on 3270 terminals sent and received whole screens or *panels*. The user saw the screen, entered some information on that screen, and hit Enter to send it back to the application.

This Cluster Controller was connected to the Mainframe in one of two ways:

- Directly by a channel.
- Indirectly through another box called a *Communications Controller* (more on these in a moment). A Cluster Controller could be connected directly to this Communications Controller or remotely over a network.

You won't see a 3270 terminal today – they're long gone. But whenever you logon to a Mainframe (unless you're logging onto UNIX Systems Services), you're actually *pretending* to be a 3270 terminal. This means that all the old Mainframe processing for 3270 terminals still works today.

> **What's a Terminal?**
>
> A keyboard and screen used to talk to a computer – to send and receive information. A terminal is like your PC, but doesn't do any actual work.
>
> You still need a terminal to talk to midrange and mainframe computers today. But instead of an actual terminal, you'll use a *terminal emulator* on your PC – software that pretends it's a terminal.

## The Traditional SNA Network

So let's put it all together... A Mainframe network (called a *subarea* network) looked a lot like Figure 13.

Your Mainframe connected via a channel to your Communications Controller (sometimes called a Front End Processor, or FEP). This was effectively a computer in its own right (starting with the 3705, then 3725, 3745 and finally 3746) that took the work of managing the network from the Mainframe. Running a program called the Network Control Program (NCP), it would connect to:

- Cluster Controllers.

- Other Communications Controllers – possibly a 'remote' Communications Controller for our Mainframe or a Communications Controller connected to another Mainframe.

- Other computer systems – like the IBM midrange iSeries® computers.

You had a couple of options about how your Communications Controller connected to the outside world including: Synchronous Data Link Control (SDLC) - the 'traditional' method, X.25, Token Ring and Ethernet.

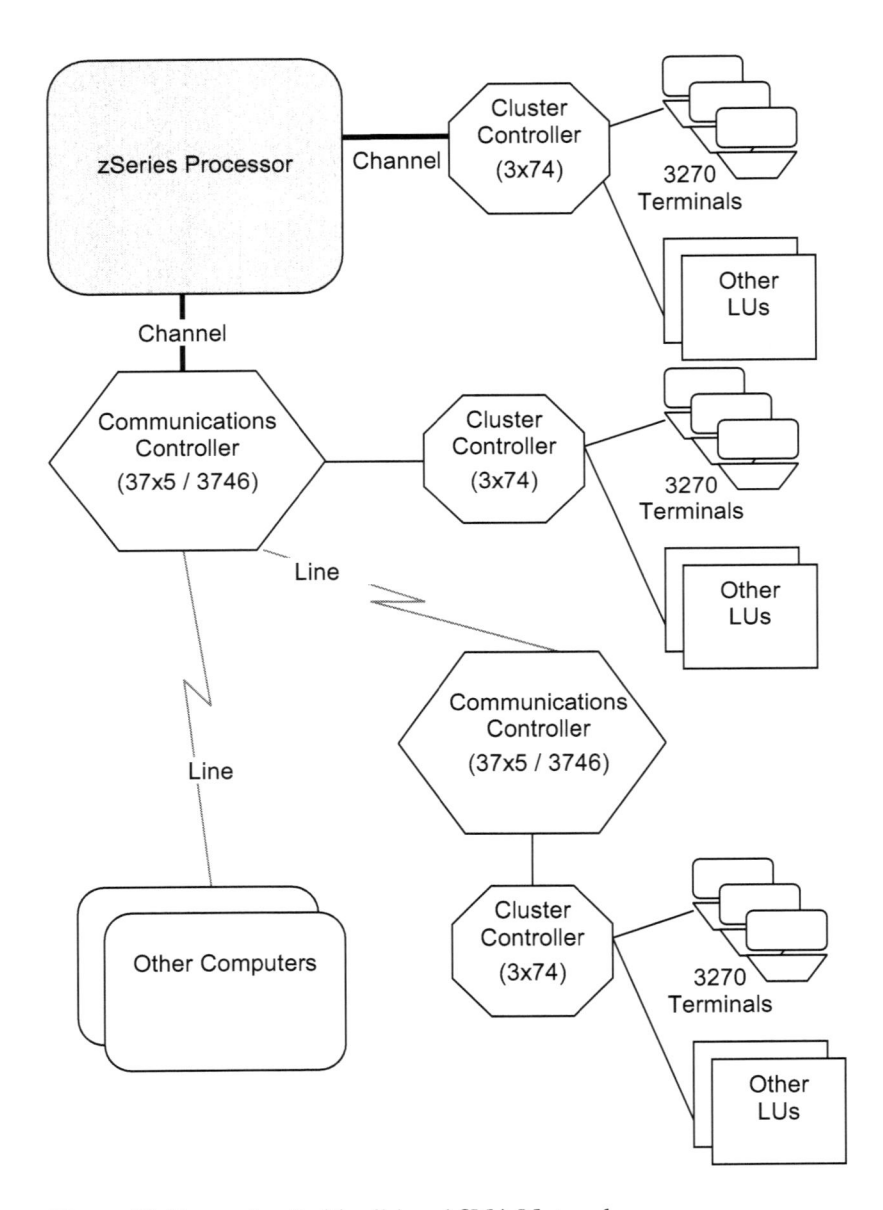

Figure 13: Example of a Traditional SNA Network

> **What's a Network?**
>
> It's a way to communicate with a computer – it can be someone on the internet, an Automated Teller Machine (ATM), or even applications programs talking to each other. Networks have a few layers:
>
> **Physical:** The physical connection, such as a phone line, a leased line, or a fiber-optic cable.
>
> **Network**: The nuts and bolts of how messages move between computers: how messages get to the computer you want, which application on the target computer to talk to, what happens if there's an error.
>
> **Application**: What format is the target application is expecting. Think of your web pages (HTML).
>
> There's a whole lot more to it (network geeks talk about the Open Systems Integration, or OSI layer – it's got seven layers), but this is a good start. SNA and TCP/IP are very much in the Network layer, though TCP/IP also has some applications.

Now, SNA had very rigid rules. Communications were done between Physical Units (PUs) that were connected by channels or network *lines*. There were a couple of different PU types - the most common being:

- Type 5 - the Mainframe processor itself.
- Type 4 - Communications Controller.
- Type 2 - Cluster Controller.

But these PUs were only the 'middle men.' Communications were actually done between *Logical Units*, or LUs. The application program was a LU, and it could talk with:

- LU Type 1 – A printer.
- LU Type 2 – A terminal (meaning the 3270).
- LU Type 3 – A printer using 3270 protocols.
- LU Type 6.2 – Another application program.

OK, so we have LUs that are connected to PUs. And these PUs communicate with other PUs over lines. So let's say that you were on a 3270 terminal and wanted to logon to CICS. Here's what happened:

Chapter 4: Talking to the Mainframe

1. You needed to manually define every LU, PU and line to the z/OS software that controls SNA: VTAM® (Virtual Telecommunications Access Method). This included the LU used by CICS.
2. You needed to *activate* every LU, PU and line. You did this by issuing a z/OS console command. This checked that everything was OK, and set the LU, PU or line ready.
3. At this point your 3270 terminal was connected to the Mainframe, but you couldn't talk to CICS yet. You had to type a command on your terminal to start a connection. When you did this the Subsystem Control Program (SSCP – part of VTAM) set up a *session* between your terminal and CICS. And away you went.

### Screen Scraping – Making Mainframe Applications Pretty

Almost every traditional Mainframe application is designed to run on a 3270 terminal. But 3270 terminals aren't as pretty as Windows on your PC.

An easy way of giving these 3270 applications a pretty Windows interface is to *screen-scrape*. Or in other words, a Windows application pretends to be a 3270 terminal. It works like this:

- The Mainframe application sends a 3270 screen. The Windows application reads and presents this screen to you as a nice Windows screen – with all the goodies you'd expect from Windows.
- You use the Windows screen to do something. The Windows application converts this to 3270 keystrokes, and sends it back to the Mainframe.

This way the Mainframe thinks it's talking to a 3270 terminal and you think you have a nice Windows application. No Mainframe programming needed.

This session remained until you logged off CICS or there was a problem on the network. If for some reason the network failed, your session failed, and you'd have to start all over again.

> ### The Other SNA
>
> Although IBM sells them as one networking method, there are actually two SNAs. The Mainframe generally uses the more traditional SNA – subarea networks. But with subarea networks, you have one boss – and you have to define every LU to that boss.
>
> This starts to breakdown when you have lots of smaller computers talking to each other – there's no boss.
>
> So IBM created Advanced Peer-to-Peer Networking® (APPN).
>
> SNA APPN networks introduce *routing* to SNA – this means that one computer can communicate with another via a third 'in-between' computer. APPN networks still have LUs and you still have to define them, but only to the APPN 'node' (the midrange or Mainframe computer) that 'owns' it.
>
> APPN networks have two new LU types: LU Type 5 (an end node, or ending point for communications) and LU Type 7 (a Network node, or intermediate point).

LUs always connected through a PU, for example a 3270 terminal through a Cluster Controller to the network. Because of this some people call SNA *hierarchical*.

OK, but what if you had more than one z/OS system sharing an SNA network? No problem - each z/OS controlled its own part of the network (and that part was called a *domain*). But before these z/OS systems could talk to each other, you needed to define and activate something called a Cross Domain Resource Manager (CDRM) to SYS1.VTAMLST. These z/OS systems didn't need Communications Controllers - they could communicate directly via a channel.

But what if they didn't share the SNA network? What if they had their own network? When SNA first came out, you couldn't communicate between one SNA network and another (for example two separate banks communicating with each other). IBM later fixed this by providing SNA Network Interconnect (SNI).

## *SNA Networks Today*

By now you're probably thinking "why the history lesson?" Well, SNA networks still work like this today, however the actual hardware has changed:

- Cluster Controllers have been replaced by PCs and UNIX computers running emulation software like Microsoft Host Integration Services.

- The Communications Controllers are now being phased out – replaced by SNA inside TCP/IP (Enterprise Extender, or EE). Or they are using software running under z/Linux that pretends to be a Communications Controller (IBM Communication Controller for Linux, or CCL).

- 3270 terminals have been replaced by 3270 emulation software.

> **TN3270 – Today's Window to the Mainframe**
>
> If you use a mainframe, you'll be using a TN3270 client of some sort.
>
> TN3270 (or Telnet 3270) is a way of sending 3270 data across a TCP/IP network. So there's no need for Communications Controllers or Cluster Controllers. All you need is PC software that supports TN3270, a TCP/IP connection to the Mainframe, and the z/OS TN3270 server up and running.

## TCP/IP Networks

If you've used the internet, you've used TCP/IP - it's become the standard networking protocol for the world. TCP/IP for Mainframes hasn't been around long, but it's making up for lost time. In many ways TCP/IP has revolutionized Mainframe networking, and traditional SNA services are being sidelined by TCP/IP.

### *What Mainframe TCP/IP Looks Like*

Let's have a look at TCP/IP on the Mainframe.

Your Mainframe will connect to your local TCP/IP network – and Figure 14 shows your choices:

- Directly to your Local Area Network (such as Ethernet) using hardware inside the Mainframe processor called the Open Systems Adapter Express (OSA Express).

- Via a router connected to the Mainframe by a channel.

- Via a channel to another Mainframe.
- Via IBM HiperSockets™ to another LPAR or z/OS image on the same physical processor. HiperSockets isn't a physical link - it's all done internally on the actual processor. However TCP/IP thinks it is - and it's very quick.

### The Oldest Box in the Room – Communications Controllers

If you were to walk into the computer room of many companies and look for the oldest piece of computer hardware, the chances are that it would be a Communications Controller.

Although they're being phased out, there are still lots of these 3745s and 3746s being used around the world. And if IBM won't look after them, there are other companies that are only too happy to help. But why keep them?

- They work. Communications Controllers have for many years been amongst the most stable and reliable hardware in the machine room. In fact, it wouldn't be unusual for your Communications Controller t be over 10 years old.
- It's a lot of work to replace them.
- It costs money to replace them. If a company decides to replace their 3745 with CCL, they need to setup a z/Linux partition, and install CCL. And CCL isn't free.
- It's a risk to replace them. Any change involves risk, and traditional SNA networks can be as essential as the Mainframe they're communicating to. So you need a good reason to change something that's working.
- Although IBM isn't selling new ones, it's still supporting them. And IBM is also still supporting the NCP software, which is also needed by CCL.

From your local TCP/IP network, you'll have one or more computers or routers to route the TCP/IP messages to other areas in your organization, or to the outside world.

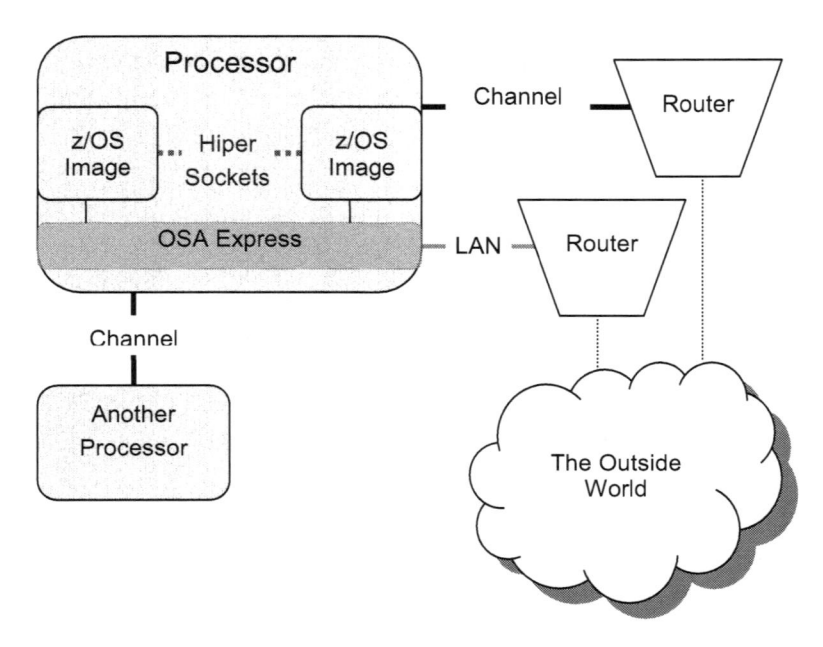

**Figure 14: A Mainframe TCP/IP Network**

## *TCP/IP vs. SNA*

TCP/IP is a lot different to SNA – in fact it's hard to be any more different. Let's compare them:

| TCP/IP | SNA |
|---|---|
| You use an IP address to specify the computer you want to talk to. An IP address is like a number like 192.144.23.10, or more recently (with TCP/IP v6) FE73:0:0:0:1:600:1587:E17B | No need to specify the computer. |
| You use a number called a port number to specify the application | You specify the LU you want to talk to – this can be hardware (like a terminal) or |

| program you want to talk to. | an application program. |
|---|---|
| Your computer doesn't need to know where the other computer is: routers and in-between computers help you here. | You manually define to the computer exactly where the other computer is, and how to get there. |
| You can talk to another computer via one or more computers or routers that are in-between. | SNA subarea networks are point to point. Only APPN networks can be routed. |
| No need for extra hardware – computers can talk directly if they have a connection. | You need PUs in between two LUs. |
| Gives you tools like File Transfer and 3270 terminal emulation. | No tools. |
| Is an 'open' networking protocol – it isn't owned by one company. | Is a 'proprietary' networking protocol – it's owned by IBM. |
| It's very easy for other computer systems like UNIX and Windows to talk to the Mainframe. | It's hard for other computer systems to talk to the Mainframe. |
| Because it's very easy to talk to the Mainframe, you need to do a lot of work to make it secure. | By its very nature, it's secure. |
| Used by almost every computer system. | Really only used by IBM Mainframe and midrange computers. |
| Your can use TCP/IP to connect your Mainframe to the Internet – so you can web-enable your Mainframe applications. | No options for connecting to the Internet. |

Chapter 4: Talking to the Mainframe

# Talking Between Applications – Middleware and SOA

Up to now we've been talking about Mainframe networking - but let's stop and have a think about your applications. OK, they just use the network facilities that SNA and TCP/IP provide - no problem. Except that people developing these applications have to think about things like:

- Where's the other application? What type of computer does it run on? How do we find it? What application are we talking to?

- Are we using SNA or TCP/IP?

- How do we know if the other application received what we sent?

- What if the other application is on a different computer platform? Do we need to convert what we're sending or what we're receiving?

- What if there's a network error – and we're in the middle of sending something?

- What if the other computer isn't working? What do we do? How would we even know?

- How can we secure the connection between our applications?

So there's a lot to think about when getting an application to talk with another application - and this isn't just a Mainframe problem.

But what if applications didn't have to worry about any of this? Just what to send (what information, and what format), what comes back (again, what information and what format), and where to send it? So the destination could be anywhere - even on a different platform.

This is exactly what Systems Oriented Architecture (SOA) is all about. Although it isn't anything concrete, SOA is a set of principles and ideas for making this happen. And there are tools that help out.

## Websphere MQ

Think of Websphere® MQ (or MQSeries® as it used to be called) as your postal service. Your application program prepares a letter, addresses it, and puts it in the post box. Websphere MQ does all the rest. It takes that letter, and makes sure that it appears in the letterbox of the receiver. Let's look at this a bit closer…

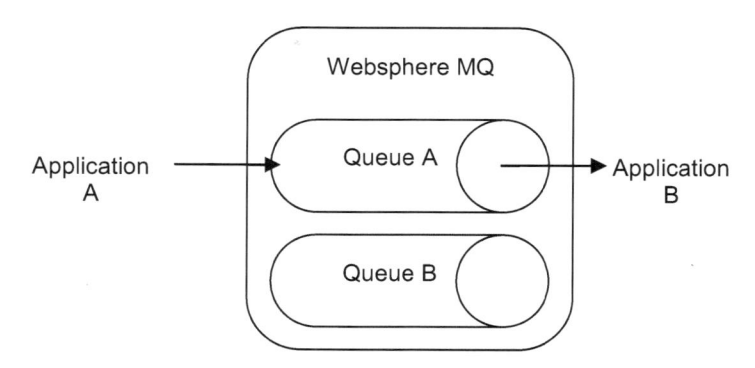

**Figure 15: Websphere MQ**

Websphere MQ consists of *queues*. So it looks something like Figure 15. Application programs use these queues to talk to each other. So in Figure 15:

- Application A puts a message on Queue A for Application B.
- Application B listens to Queue A, and processes the message when it receives it.

Well, that's all great, but how does this help? Websphere MQ takes over:

- **Message Delivery.** Applications don't have to worry about how the messages get to the destination – Websphere MQ figures this out.

- **Message Integrity.** Applications don't have to worry about whether a message gets through – Websphere MQ looks after queue integrity.

- **Availability**. Application A doesn't have to worry about whether Application B is up or down. If Application B is down, it can check the queue when it comes back up - Websphere MQ will keep it there ready.

- **Message security**. Websphere MQ can be tailored so that only the right application can see messages on a queue.

But it goes a bit further than that:

- Application A doesn't have to know anything about Application B, except the format of messages to be sent to Application B. So Application B can be running in IMS or CICS, it could be on z/OS or UNIX, it could be written in Java or COBOL. Application A doesn't care. This also makes it a lot easier to migrate Application B to a different computer system or platform.

- Websphere MQ lets applications *share* queues – even if they're running on different z/OS systems. So you could have two computer systems running Application B. If one system is shutdown, the other can service the queue.

Websphere MQ doesn't just run on the Mainframe, but runs quite happily on other platforms like UNIX. So it's great for inter-platform communications.

## *Simple Object Access Protocol*

With Websphere MQ, messages are like mailing a letter - you don't often wait for a response. Simple Object Access Protocol (SOAP) is a bit different - it's usually used by applications requesting services. So they send a request and wait for a response.

SOAP isn't actually a software product - it's more a framework for applications talking to each other using 'standard' web technology.

SOAP information uses a standard format called XML (Extensible Markup Language). It usually uses HTTP (Hypertext Transfer Protocol. The protocol you use for the internet) for sending messages back and forth, though it can also use Websphere MQ. Using this standard web technology means that anything that can use the internet can use SOAP - no extra software needed!

People are seeing SOAP as a great way of web-enabling old Mainframe applications – letting web applications access existing data and applications. IBM agrees with them, and has been spending a lot of effort to support SOAP on their Mainframe systems – including IMS, CICS and Websphere Application Server.

Some people use the terms SOA and SOAP interchangeably, but be careful. They're not the same thing.

## *Enterprise Service Bus*

You'll often hear people talking about the Enterprise Service Bus, or ESB. Well, it's hard to believe but the ESB isn't real. It's a concept of a central highway that your middleware uses to send messages between applications. But you can buy software that sits where the ESB is - between your applications. Some people believe that this software is really the ESB.

So what does this software do? Here are some examples:

- Change the address (routing). This can help when the original destination is unavailable, and a different one is running the application.

- Changing the protocol (mediation). The destination application may have been completely changed, and it no longer receives the original protocol.

- Changing the message. For example language translation, or changing the format of the message (because the destination application has changed).

- Help manage messages in and out. There are many ways to do this, including monitoring and logging messages (so you know how many were sent, when they were sent, who sent them, and how long they took).

ESB software gives you a way of monitoring and controlling middleware messages, which can be very handy as your middleware environment gets more and more complicated. Some examples include IBM Websphere Enterprise Service Bus and TIBCO Enterprise Message Service™.

## The Last Word

So the traditional Mainframe networks (SNA subarea) are slowly being taken over by TCP/IP – yet SNA is still a critical part of most Mainframe systems. Even so, the TCP/IP juggernaut keeps on rolling on. And Websphere MQ is becoming more and more popular as more and more applications on different platforms want to talk to each other.

# Chapter 5: Putting the Mainframe to Work - Database and Transaction Managers

Mainframes do commercial data processing – putting a piece of data into a database, looking at the data, taking it out. Any organization with a lot of very large databases and a lot of reasons to access them quickly is a potential Mainframe user.

For large scale database related applications you're going to need two things: a Database Manager and a Transaction Manager.

## The Database Manager – Your Database Nanny

We know what you're thinking… "Why do I need a Database Manager? Why can't I just write a program to access the database?" Well, databases are fragile things. So if you don't want them broken, you need something to look after them - a database 'nanny.' In fact people are amazed at the work a Database Manager does. Let's look at the nanny's job description.

# Task 1: Data Integrity - Preventing the Database from Being Hurt.

Let's look at something that's very important to you: your bank account. The balance of this account (together with a whole lot of other information) will be stored as a number somewhere in a database. If you take money out of your account, this number will change. Now you know that this number is important to you – if it suddenly becomes zero, you've got no cash.

To the bank it's even more important. If it can't rely on this number being right, it can't do business. If *you* can't rely on this number being right, you'll go to another bank. Your bank needs this number to survive. This is the number one job of a Database Manager –*database integrity*. So how does it do it? Let's look at the top ways to corrupt a database.

## How to Corrupt a Database 1: Two people changing it at the same time

Let's say that you're at an ATM withdrawing some of your hard earned money – Program A will be doing this work. However at the same time the bank is transferring money you won in a competition into your bank account – using Program W. When you withdraw money a computer program will get your balance, subtract the amount you withdrew, and then put this number back into your bank account. That's the *transaction*. So consider this:

- Program A gets your bank balance.
- Program W gets your balance.
- Program W puts back your new balance (with all your winnings).
- Program A puts back your new balance (less the amount you withdrew).

Oops! Your winnings have effectively been wiped out by Program A. There goes that new car!

To stop this, we need to have a *locking* mechanism:

- Program A gets the lock on your bank account then gets your bank balance.
- Program W tries to get the lock on your bank account, but has to wait.
- Program A puts back your new balance (less the amount you withdrew), and releases the lock on your account.
- Program W now gets the lock, and gets your bank balance.
- Program W puts back your new balance (including all your winnings), and releases the lock on your account.

And voila! You're ready to buy that new car.

Most operating systems stop two tasks from accessing the same file or dataset at the same time. But to provide this kind of locking for individual records is a lot harder. Sounds like a job for the Database Manager.

## How to Corrupt a Database 2: Security Failure.

It's every bank's nightmare – a security failure. This is where Mainframes start to look really good – computers don't come more secure than Mainframes. But database security isn't just stopping people from outside getting to the databases. It can also mean things like:

- Stopping test programs from accidentally accessing production data.
- Stopping programs accidentally accessing data in the wrong database.

So database management systems will have a system of securing the databases – to the level where some programs or users can access some databases (or even records), but not others.

## How to Corrupt a Database 3: Computer Failure.

Let's go back to you winning that competition. Congratulations, we're transferring money from another account into yours:

1. Program W updates the bank account of the competition holder and takes out the money.
2. Program W puts this money into your bank account.

> **What's a Transaction?**
> It's a piece of work. If you transfer money from one bank account to another, an application program will have to do several things - possibly to different databases. All of these steps together are one transaction.

But what happens if something goes wrong in between these two steps? Say Program W fails? Or someone hits the power switch on the computer? Or the disk drive where the database lives suddenly becomes full? All that money destined for your bank account has disappeared.

So a Database Manager needs to be able to handle this. It does this by detecting (or being told by the Transaction Manager) that something's wrong, and undoing Step 1. We call this *rolling back in-flight transactions*. So everything is as it was before the transaction started.

### How to Corrupt a Database 4: Application Program Failure.

What if an application program that updates the database goes crazy – and starts overwriting database information? There's not much a database management system can do about this. What it can do is provide a way of finding out later what happened, and even to backout these changes. This is where *journaling* and *logging* come in.

## Task 2: Journaling and Logging - Who's Been Visiting my Database?

What on earth are *journaling* and *logging*? What's the difference between the two? You sometimes hear these terms used interchangeably, but generally speaking:

***Journaling***: Keeping records of who has done what in order to *backout* or *roll forward*. Now, we've already talked a bit about backout: undoing changes when something's gone wrong. Roll forward is the opposite - updating a database after it has been restored with all the changes that have happened *since the backup occurred*. This is also called *forward recovery*.

***Logging:*** Keeping records of who has done what for audit purposes. This way you can go back and say to Bank Teller A: "why did you record a very large withdrawal from account X and then try to catch a plane to a tropical paradise with a suitcase full of money?"

---

**Database and Transaction Managers on Other Platforms**

Database Managers and Transaction Managers don't just run on Mainframes. Some Database Managers on other systems are:

- Microsoft SQL Server®.
- MySQL®.
- Oracle® Database.

Packages like Microsoft Access™ roll the work of a Transaction Manager and Database Manager into one.

Some Transaction Managers are:

- SAP Web Application Server Java
- Oracle Tuxedo™.

---

Some database management systems use one system for both, others have separate systems.

## Task 3: Concurrent Access - Who Do We Let Visit Our Database?

*Concurrent Access* is a fancy term for letting many different people access databases at the same time. We've already talked about locking so a database can't be corrupted by two programs trying to update a record at the same time. But we also need to let as many programs as possible access the database at the same time. This means letting two programs update different records in the same database simultaneously, programs that could be running on different machines.

## Task 4: Backup and Recovery - Database Health Care

When your databases are important to you, you want to have plans in case something goes wrong – *Disaster Recovery Plans*. These plans will include backing up your databases. Every site on the planet performs regular backups of critical databases. But what's even more important is being able to recover your databases. You need to test this, and test it regularly (we talk about Disaster Recovery in Chapter 9).

In days past, to backup your databases you had to stop anyone accessing them, run your backups (which could run for hours), then let everyone at them again. Today people pay money for Mainframes because they want access 24 hours a day, seven days a week. So database systems generally give you a way of backing up your databases *while they're still being used*.

## Task 5: Performance - Fitness for Databases

Not only do you want your databases to have perfect integrity, be secure, and be accessible by lots of people at the same time. You also want to access them *fast*. Database Managers can supply ways to help you with:

- **Buffering and Caching**: A lot of Database Managers store some of your database in memory to make it faster to access. This can give you amazing performance improvements.

- **Performance Tools**: Tools to analyze your database performance and even recommend changes.

## Task 6: Hide the Databases

That's right – Database Managers hide the physical structure of the databases. The application programs only see a *logical view* of the databases. So an application may see just one database when it's really several databases spread over different disks. This lets the Database Administrator do anything needed to improve performance and availability – without applications needing to know.

## Task 7: Utilities

There are so many jobs that you need to do with your databases. Your friendly Database Manager will give you utilities to make these jobs easier, including:

- **Copying Databases**: Sounds simple but some databases may be spread across many files on different disks. So a utility that makes copying databases easier is great.

- **Defragment Databases:** In many database systems your databases can get fragmented with use – meaning the data gets spread all over the place. This can make your databases bigger than they need to be and affect their performance. So you'll need to defragment them regularly.

- **Create Databases:** Yes, creating databases isn't necessarily straightforward. You may also want to create indexes – a different way of looking at your database that can speed up performance.

- **Find Out Information:** Such as, "how big is Database A?" or "is Database B open and available?" This can be in the form of a screen that you access or an Application Programming Interface (API), or both.

- **Checking the Structure of a Database:** Checking it hasn't been damaged or corrupted.

So, you can see that a Database Manager (sometimes called a DBMS or *Database Management System*) has a lot of work to do. But he's only half the team – let's look at the *Transaction Manager*.

# The Transaction Manager – Crowd Management

Picture this: the biggest football game of the year is on this week, and tickets have just gone on sale. Everyone wants a ticket – but only club members are eligible. You're in charge of the ticket sales – and there's a huge crowd swarming around your ticket booths trying to buy them.

The Transaction Manager manages that crowd. Let's look at some of his problems:

## Problem 1: Keeping the Crowd Happy

You don't want an angry crowd, so you need to create an environment where everyone's happy. You might decide to have multiple ticket sales booths, infrastructure where there are orderly lines (and no-one can push in – we hate people that push in), maybe have some stalls selling soft drinks and food – perhaps even a band for atmosphere.

Transaction Managers do kind of the same things for programs. They provide ways to:

- **Talk to Database Managers:** (Ticket sales booths).
- **Ensure Data Integrity:** We've already talked about this for Database Managers but what if a transaction transfers money from a bank account stored in an IMS database to an account stored in a DB2 database? If the transaction dies half way through, the Transaction Manager needs to tell both IMS and DB2 to backout any changes made.
- **Speed up Transactions:** Suppose someone is at a ticket booth paying with a credit card, which takes some time. You'd be smart to move that person to one side while the credit card is being processed, and look after the next customer (you can come back to that first customer after the credit card processing is done). In computer terms, if a program is waiting for something to happen (like a database access), you can move it to one side and process the next program.

**Prioritize Transactions**: What if there are different classes of members? Say gold members get served before green members? Some Transaction Managers let you assign priorities to programs. So a program with a higher priority is run first.

> **Transactions and the ACID Test**
>
> You may hear people talking about **ACID** transactions. By this they're really talking about a set of rules that Transaction Managers should follow:
>
> **Atomicity**: If a transaction updates multiple databases, the Transaction Managers should be able to guarantee that all are updated, or none are: data integrity.
>
> **Consistency**: A transaction should never be half completed.
>
> **Isolation**: No-one can see data in a half changed state. Either they see it before it's changed or after the transaction has finished.
>
> **Durability**: Once the transaction is complete the transaction's updates cannot be *undone*.
>
> Putting it this way is relatively new, but Mainframe Transaction Managers have been doing it for decades.

## Problem 2: Only Members Get to Buy Tickets

You guessed it, Transaction Managers have security. Now you're probably thinking "why do they bother? Database Managers handle security." That's true, but most organizations use the Transaction Manager to define who can run which transaction, and setup the Database Manager so that the Transaction Manager can do anything it wants. Transactions generally equate to a business function, so it's easier to decide who can do what here. Databases are harder - they can be used by many different transactions.

## Problem 3: Cleanup When Things Go Wrong

Things always go wrong – someone in the crowd spills a drink, or someone buys a ticket and then changes their mind. Transaction Managers need to handle these problems. For example:

- **A program crashes.** The Transaction Manager needs to detect this and cleanup anything that needs to be cleaned up – and this will include telling a Database Manager to roll-back any in-flight transactions. It may also need to let someone know that the program has crashed and provide diagnostic tools so that the problem can be fixed.

- **One part of a transaction can't complete**. We've touched on this before. Say you've got a transaction that updates two databases on different machines: Database A and Database B. To keep integrity, we can update both or neither – never just one (this is called an *atomic transaction*). If you've updated Database A but can't update Database B, the Transaction Manager needs to tell the Database Manager to backout the Database A update.

- **A program loops.** If a program is just looping and doing nothing, it can consume resources and stop other programs from running. Some Transaction Managers handle this, and will crash the program if it runs for too long.

- **Communications are lost**. A user starts something, and then we lose communications with them. Or an application program wants to access a database but can no longer talk to the Database Manager.

## *Problem 4: Batch*

What if a corporate sponsor is entitled to a lot of tickets? If this sponsor came to your ticket booth and spent an hour buying all the tickets they want, other people in the queue are going to be very, very upset – and no amount of soft drink vendors will be able to change that. You need a way to sell these tickets (in batch) to the corporate sponsor without affecting the other work.

Many Transaction Managers are faced with this problem. In the past you often had to shutdown a Transaction Manager to run batch. Today most Transaction Managers have a facility whereby you can perform batch without impacting normal operations.

## *Problem 5: How Many Tickets Are Left?*

Let's say that members can only buy two tickets. You need to keep track of how many tickets each member has bought. You also need to know how many have been sold, and how many are left.

Transaction Managers usually keep a log of what's happened. This log may include:

- Who used which application program.
- Who tried to use an application program but wasn't allowed to.
- How many times an application program accessed a database.
- How many resources were used by each application program (like how much processor, memory, I/O).
- How long each application program took.

From this information you can diagnose problems, assess performance, figure out if a bigger machine is needed, and perform a security audit.

Transaction Managers usually (but not necessarily) provide an *application environment* – meaning an environment where application programs can run. Similarly *application servers* (that provide an application environment) often provide the services of a Transaction Manager. We talk more about application environments in the next chapter.

So, the Transaction Manager (sometimes called a transaction processor or TP) controls the crowd of transactions coming in.

## Transaction and Database Managers on z/OS

Mainframes have been doing transaction and database management for decades – longer than anything else on the market. So you would think they're good at it, and they are. But more importantly, they've been processing huge workloads and managing critical data for decades. You may hear a lot of people arguing about this, but the bottom line is that nothing does large scale transaction and database management like the Mainframe. Let's have a look at the stars that achieve this.

# IMS – Transaction and Database Manager

Information Management System (IMS™) was the very first database management system for the Mainframe. And would you believe, it started life as part of the NASA Apollo Space Program (though it wasn't called IMS then). With its glamorous start to life, IMS was around before z/OS (it first ran on the System/360 machines).

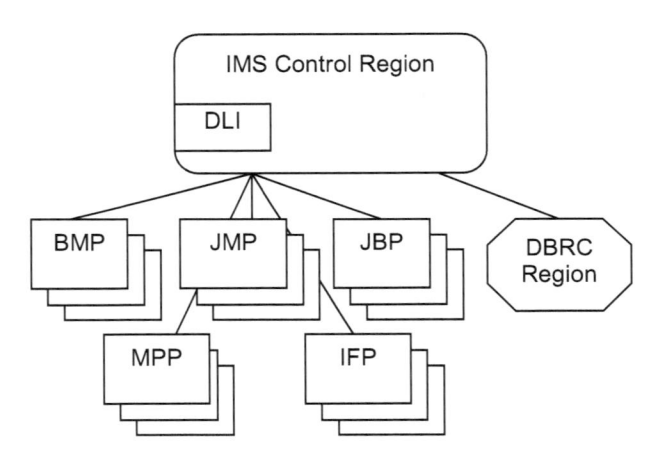

**Figure 16: An IMS Subsystem**

IMS is both a Transaction Manager and a Database Manager. Today, you can run IMS:

- As a Transaction Manager (we call this a DCCTL region, or Data Communications Control).

- As a Database Manager (DBCTL – DataBase Control).

- As both (DB/DC or TM/DB – Transaction Manager/Database).

## What IMS Looks Like

Figure 16 show a typical IMS subsystem consisting of a couple of different address spaces or *regions*:

**Control Region:** The boss of the enterprise.

**Database Recovery and Control (DBRC) Region**: In charge of logging and the Recovery ConTrol (RECON) datasets (which hold everything you need to recover your databases).

**DLI Region (DLISAS)**: Handles access to DL/I databases (but not Fastpath). This address space is optional, and some sites don't have one (in this case the work is done by the Control Region). You won't see this region for IMS DCCTL subsystems.

**Regions Where Application Programs Run:** IMS subsystems have several separate address spaces where the application programs actually run:

- Message Processing Regions (MPP): Online programs.
- Batch Message Processing (BMP): Batch jobs accessing IMS databases.
- Java Message Processing Regions (JMP): The same as MPP regions, but for Java programs.
- Java Batch Processing Regions (JBP): The same as BMP regions, but for Java programs.
- IMS Fastpath Processing (IFP) Regions: The same as MPP regions, but for programs accessing Fastpath databases (we talk about Fastpath soon).

You won't see any of these regions (except BMP and JBP) for DBCTL subsystems.

When you start IMS, you start the IMS Control Region which automatically starts all the others.

There's another way you can run IMS which doesn't have all of these address spaces – an IMS DBB region. This is a standalone IMS batch job – everything is done in the one address space. It's called a DBB region because that's the parameter you use to tell IMS it's running in batch.

Chapter 5: Putting the Mainframe to Work

## IMS Support Address Spaces

You can also find some supporting address spaces for IMS, looking a lot like Figure 17.

**Internal Resource Locking Manager (IRLM)**: Lets IMS sub-systems share databases.

**Common Queue Server (CQS)**: Lets IMS sub-systems share queues. This allows different IMS sub-systems to share transaction workloads (so if one IMS is too busy, a second can process a transaction).

**Fast Database Recovery (FDBR)**: If an IMS sub-system fails while it's in the middle of a transaction, then other IMS sub-systems sharing resources (like databases) may be locked out. The FDBR region detects any failure and performs any cleanup work (like rolling out in-flight transactions), clearing the way for other IMS sub-systems to keep working.

> **What's an IMSPlex?**
> A group of IMS subsystems talking to each other over a Parallel Sysplex.

**IMS Connect**: Brings your IMS sub-system to the internet. You use IMS Connect to web enable IMS programs and let Websphere Application Server use IMS.

**Structured Call Interface (SCI)**: Manage Communications between IMS sub-systems in an IMSPlex.

**Operations Manager (OM)**: A central point for issuing IMS commands for multiple IMS sub-systems in an IMSPlex.

**Resource Manager (RM)**: Manage resources and coordinate resource changes for all IMS sub-systems in an IMSPlex.

None of these support address spaces are compulsory – you'll only have them if you need them.

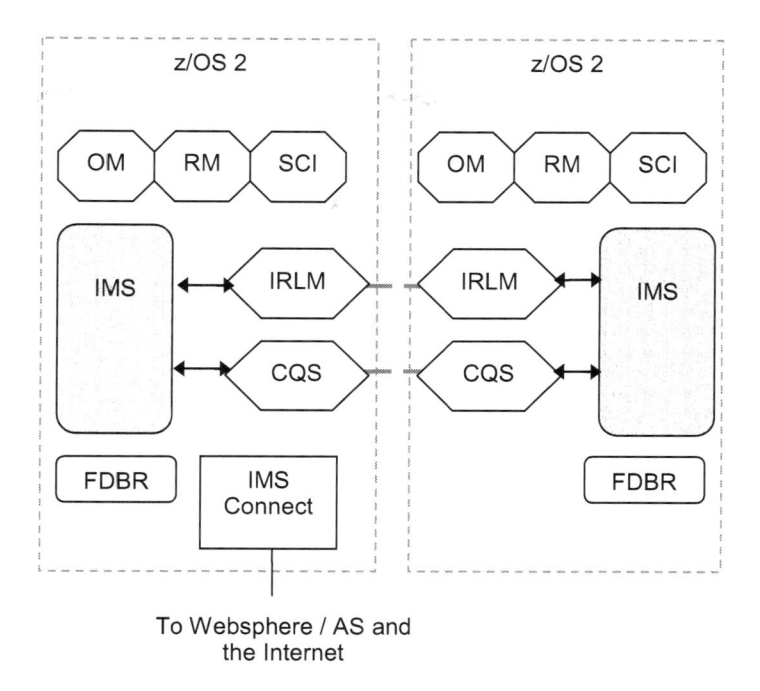

Figure 17: IMS and IMS Supporting Address Spaces

## IMS as a Database Manager (IMS DB)

IMS databases probably hold more critical data than anything else on the planet - including a lot of bank accounts (possibly including yours). And get this: nothing's faster than IMS.

Now IMS has two main database types:

- **Full Function:** The older type – also known as DL/I databases.
- **Fastpath**: A 'newer' and faster type.

Both are what are called *hierarchical* databases – a different way of organizing a database to the *relational* idea used by just about every other widely used database system. Being hierarchical generally means that (all things being equal) IMS is faster, but it's a lot harder to get at the information. With relational databases you can just use a different

Chapter 5: Putting the Mainframe to Work                                95 *query* to find different information (or information in a different form). But with hierarchical databases, the chances are you're going to have to make a change to the database design itself.

Let's see some of the highlights of IMS DB:

- It is regarded as the most robust and secure Database Manager in the world.
- You can backup IMS databases while they're still being used using Online Image Copy.
- You can reorganize IMS databases while they're still being used.
- IMS Database Managers running on different z/OS systems can share an IMS database using the Inter-Region Lock Manager (IRLM).
- An individual IMS database can be up to 40 Terabytes in size. That's a *really* big database.
- You can access IMS databases from IMS TM, Websphere Application Server or CICS.

The problem with IMS databases are:

- It's harder to create and maintain IMS databases than other Database Managers.
- Because IMS databases are harder to manage, there aren't too many new IMS database being created – people are looking elsewhere (like to DB2) for their new databases.

## IMS as a Transaction Manager (IMS TM)

IMS is just great at managing transactions. It provides:

- An application environment.
- Transaction prioritization.
- The best application program separation – because application programs actually run in their own separate address space.

What On Earth is a Mainframe?

- A way to run batch jobs against IMS databases at the same time as your normal work (BMPs) – no need to shut down.
- A way to access both IMS and DB2 databases.
- It supports COBOL, Assembler, PL/1 and Java – that's right, you can write Java applications that run within IMS.
- It supplies a couple of ways of web-enabling IMS applications:
    - Using IMS Connect to connect to Websphere Application Server.
    - Using Websphere MQ to connect to Websphere Application Server.
    - Using the IMS Connect and the IMS SOAP Gateway to accept SOAP requests.
- It can handle huge number of transactions without breaking into a sweat. IBM has benchmarked an IMS system processing 22,000 transactions *per second*.
- Different IMS TM regions running on different z/OS systems can share queues (meaning transactions coming in and responses going out). This helps you balance your transaction load between IMS regions.

### Codd and the Birth of Relational Databases

Today just about every Database Manager you find manages *relational* databases – an idea first put forward in 1969 by Edgar 'Ted' Codd when working on Mainframes with IBM.

A relational database is made up of tables that are related. So one table may hold customer data, a second may hold customer bank accounts, and be related to the first by the customer ID.

An Oxford trained mathematician, Codd joined IBM in 1949. But when he proposed his relational database system in 1969 IBM wasn't convinced - they already had a database manager: IMS. Codd eventually got his way, and DB2 was announced by IBM in 1983.

The problems with IMS TM are:

Chapter 5: Putting the Mainframe to Work                    97

- It's far more difficult to write application programs than other application servers.

- It's more complicated to setup and run.

- Although there are ways to web enable your IMS applications, you need extra software (like IMS Connect) – so it's not straightforward.

## DB2 – Database Manager

DB2® is IBM's relational Database Manager. Being relational makes it easier to create and manage the databases, and to write applications to access them. So the chances are that if you're writing a new application for the Mainframe, you'll be using DB2.

### What DB2 Looks Like

Look at a typical DB2 subsystem in Figure 18. From here, you can see that DB2 is really five main address spaces:

**System Services**: The brains of the organization, it does all the main tasks like:

- Talking with clients accessing the database.

- Looking after logging.

**Database Services:** This handles requests to the databases. It handles security and does a bit of magic to improve performance.

**Inter-Region Locking Manager (IRLM)**: This looks after database locking (so multiple DB2 subsystems can share databases).

**Distributed Data Facility Services (DDF):** This talks to other database subsystems that support DRDA (Distributed Relational Database Architecture – a standard for relational Database Managers to talk to each other). If you don't need to talk to other database subsystems, then you don't need this address space.

```
         Applications
    ┌────────────────────┐
    │ CICS               │
    │  ┌───────────────┐ │
    │  │ IMS           │ │
    │  │  ┌──────────┐ │ │              DB2              IRLM ─── To Other DB2s
    │  │  │ Websphere│ │ │           System                  
    │  │  │ ┌───────┐│ │ │           Services          DDF  ─── To Other DBMS
    │  │  │ │ Batch ││ │ │
    │  │  │ │ ┌────┐││ │ │                             DB2
    │  │  │ │ │TSO/E│││ │ │                         Database
    │  │  │ │ └────┘││ │ │                         Services
    └────────────────────┘
    ┌────────────────┐
    │ DB2 SPAS       │                                DB2
    │                │                              Databases
    └────────────────┘
```

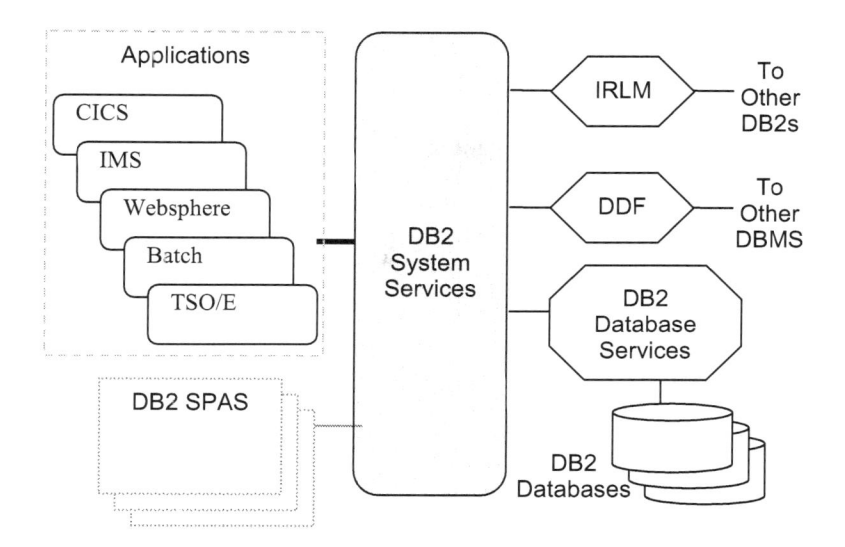

**Figure 18: A DB2 Subsystem**

**Stored Procedures Address Space (SPAS)**: This is where stored procedures run. Stored procedures are like 'mini-programs' that are actually stored in DB2 databases themselves. Using stored procedures can improve performance and make application development easier. If you don't use stored procedures, you don't need SPAS. You can also have more than one SPAS.

## Six Things You Need to Know About DB2

1. DB2 runs on lots of different platforms (like UNIX and Windows), not just z/OS.

2. DB2 subsystems can share databases using DDF.

3. You can backup DB2 databases while they're still being used – no need to shut them down.

4. Like all relational databases, your application programs use a language called *Structured Query Language* (SQL) to tell DB2 what it wants to do with the database.

5. You can look at and update data in DB2 from TSO/ISPF using something called SPUFI (SQL Processing User File Input), or

using a separate product called IBM QMF™ (Query Management Facility). These utilities won't replace application programs, but give Database Administrators a way to access and manage the data (we talk about Database Administrators later).

6. The actual DB2 data is stored in VSAM datasets called *tablespaces*. You can have one or more tablespaces making up a DB2 table, and one or more DB2 tables making up a DB2 database. DB2 also has *indexes* (a way of quickly finding a record) and *views* (a different way of looking at the data).

## *CICS – Transaction Manager and a Bit More*

IBM CICS® started life in 1968 as a 'terminal manager,' meaning it ran applications that talked to people using terminals. Programmers didn't have to worry about the details of communicating with terminals, and also got a way to access datasets at no extra cost. IBM didn't think CICS would last long, and in 1968 it was free.

CICS is a whole lot different today.

### What CICS Looks Like

CICS runs in just one address space. However many organizations choose to share the work across several separate CICS regions that talk to each other - Figure 19 shows how this works.

- The Terminal Owning Regions (TORs) manage the 3270 terminals.

- The File Owning Regions (FORs) manage VSAM files (we'll talk more about this in a second).

- The Application Owning Regions (AORs) do all the rest.

- You can have as many TORs, AORs and FORs as you want.

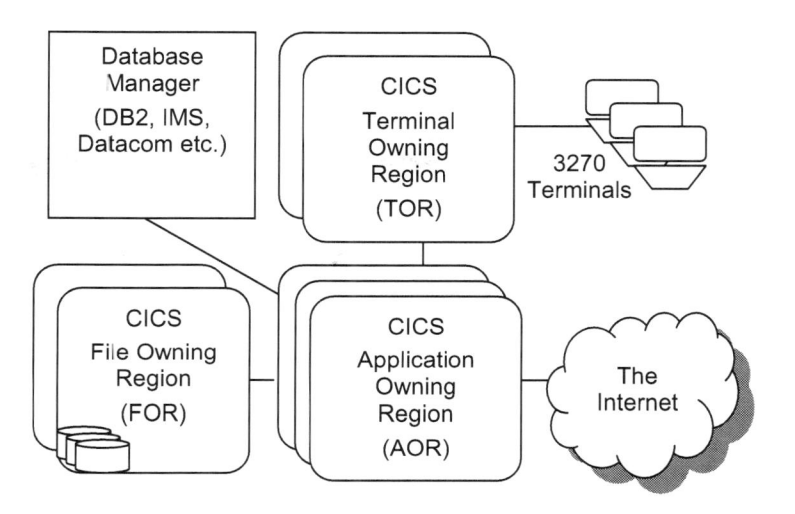

**Figure 19: Connected CICS Regions**

So why separate your regions? There are a couple of reasons:

- One CICS region can only do so much work. So splitting into several different CICS regions increases the amount of work that can be done. You can even share work across different z/OS systems.

- You can separate your applications. So if one application causes problems with a CICS region, it won't affect any other applications.

Big sites will have lots of CICS regions – there are some sites that run hundreds. So managing these CICS regions becomes lots of work. IBM has tried to make this easier with IBM CICSPlex® Systems Manager (CPSM) (a CICSPlex is a group of CICS regions that talk with each other over a Parallel Sysplex). So a site using CPSM would look like Figure 20.

**CMAS - The Controlling MAS:** This is a CICS region that is only used to manage other CICS regions on the z/OS system in the same CICSPlex - you need one per z/OS.

**MAS:** A normal CICS region.

**CAS:** An address space that lets you manage the CICSPlex using a TSO/ISPF program – you only need one per CICSPlex – but it has to run in the same z/OS as the TSO you're using.

**WUI - Web User Interface:** This lets you manage the CICSPlex from a web browser. You only need one per CICSPlex.

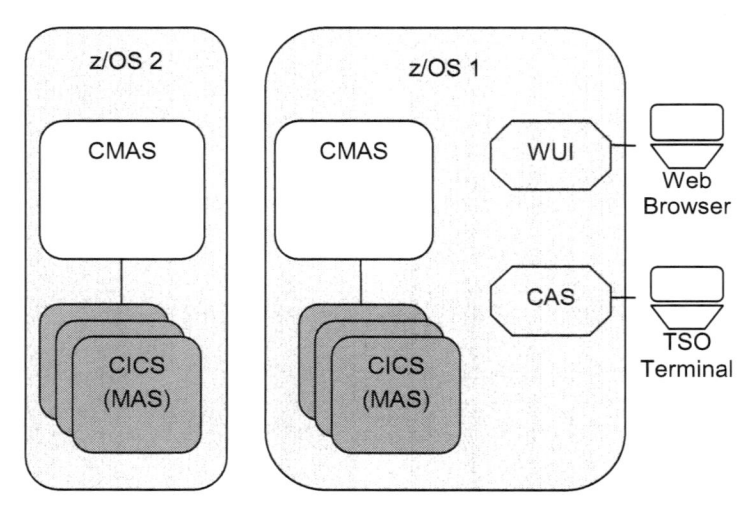

**Figure 20: A CICSPlex**

## CICS as a Transaction Manager
CICS provides:

- An application environment that is much easier to use than the IMS application environment.

- Transaction prioritization – important transactions run first.

- A way to run CICS programs from outside of CICS (for example, from a batch job).

- Logging and journaling.

### Confused Over CICS?

CICS – it's just four letters, but the name's been changing:

- CICS/VS in 1973.
- CICS/MVS® in 1987.
- CICS/ESA® in 1989.
- CICS TS in 1994.

The versions have also been changing:

- 1.x for CICS/VS.
- 2.x for CICS/MVS.
- 3.x and 4.x for CICS/ESA.
- **1.x for CICS TS.**

That's right. The versions 'reset' in 1994 when the name changed to CICS TS. However we all still call it CICS - only we like to pronounce it differently:

- In the US – 'see eye see ess'.
- In the UK and Australia – 'kicks'.
- In Spain – 'seecs'.

---

- Most z/OS Database Managers provide a way for CICS programs to use them, including DB2, IMS, CA-Datacom and Adabas.
- It supports COBOL, Assembler, PL/1 and Java.
- It supplies a couple of ways of web-enabling CICS applications:
    - Using CICS Transaction Manager to connect to Websphere Application Server.
    - CICS programs can process and send SOAP requests directly.

- o CICS is a web server. Yes, you can publish web pages straight from CICS. And CICS programs can dynamically create them.
- CICS transactions can be shared across CICS systems – both on the same z/OS systems or different ones.

## CICS as a Database Manager

CICS was never designed to be a Database Manager. However it has slowly been improved over the years, so it now gives a lot of Database Manager functionality for VSAM datasets – call it a Database Manager Lite. CICS provides:

- A way for CICS application programs to access VSAM datasets.
- Locking of individual records – both from tasks running within CICS, and from other tasks (if you setup z/OS's VSAM Record Level Sharing).
- Journaling of changes to VSAM records.
- Security.
- Logging of activity.
- Some performance improvements.

It doesn't provide:

- A way for non-CICS programs to access VSAM records using CICS services. Only CICS programs can do this (though you can run CICS programs outside of CICS).
- A way to forward recover VSAM datasets from CICS journals. You need another product like IBM CICS VSAM Recovery.
- An insulating layer between the application and the physical structure of the database.

In general, CICS VSAM isn't great at handling really large databases or the huge workloads that IMS and DB2 eat up for breakfast. You'd normally expect to see smaller applications using CICS/VSAM.

### Why Have IMS *AND* CICS?

It can seem like a big mystery. Why does IBM have both IMS TM and CICS – don't they do the same thing? The answer: history.

IMS started out as a Database and Transaction Manager – but not for terminal applications. That's right - IMS actually talking to humans (on a terminal or computer screen) came later. CICS started life as a terminal manager – letting people on a terminal access files. See the difference? But it goes further.

**IMS**

- Included a full function Database Manager.
- Had excellent application program separation – one program couldn't affect another (or IMS itself).
- Didn't handle terminals or terminal screens very well.
- Application programming was more difficult.

**CICS:**

- Didn't have a Database Manager – accessing databases came later.
- Ran everything in the same address space – so one application program could write over another program's memory (or CICS's memory for that matter). So it wasn't as robust.
- Handled terminals and terminals screens very well.
- Application programming was easier.

Over the years, development of both CICS and IMS has solved a lot of these problems, and in doing so has closed the gap between the two. However because of history (and existing applications), IBM still sells and supports both.

## *Websphere Application Server*

If you want to write a new web enabled application running on the Mainframe, the chances are you'll be writing it to run under Websphere Application Server. Websphere Application Server (or Websphere AS) is the new kid on the block. But it's not only an application environment, it's also a Transaction Manager.

> ### What is Websphere?
> 
> It seems there's a thousand different Webspheres out there. But Websphere's really a group of IBM products that run on z/OS and other platforms. For z/OS it includes:
> 
> - Websphere Application Server.
> - Websphere MQ: Messaging software.
> - Websphere Developer for z/OS: An application development environment.
> - Websphere Enterprise Service Bus: Web services management.
> - Websphere Host Access Transformation Services: For 3270 screen scrapers (meaning programs that pretend to be a 3270 terminal).
> - Websphere Studio Workload Simulator: Simulate production workloads for your testing of z/OS web services applications.
> - Websphere Studio Application Monitor: Monitor Websphere application performance.

Websphere AS not only runs on the Mainframe, it runs on other platforms as well. But perhaps the best thing about Websphere AS is that it looks the same to developers on all platforms. Someone who can develop on Websphere AS on Windows can do a lot of development on the Mainframe without learning anything new.

## *What Websphere Application Server Looks Like*

Have a look at a typical Websphere AS setup in Figure 21. The Controller Region is the brains of the organization, and is managed by a console that runs on any web browser. It attaches to one or more Server Regions, which is where your applications actually run. All outside access is managed by the Controller Region, including access to other Transaction and Database Managers.

## *What Websphere AS Gives*

It gives a Java 2 Enterprise Edition (J2EE™) environment – or in other words an environment that runs Java programs, and can accept requests from other programs. In a nutshell, you get three main things with Websphere AS:

- An HTTP Server: You can host web pages.

- Web Services Support: So web applications can talk to Websphere AS applications, asking for and providing information.

- Connectors to Database Managers: Allowing Websphere AS applications to access databases.

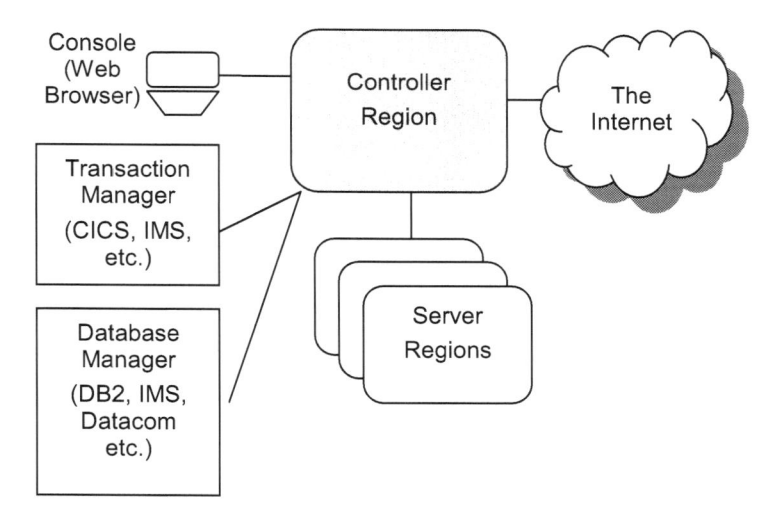

Figure 21: Websphere Application Server Setup

## Other Transaction and Database Managers

We've really only talked about the IBM products on the market, and that's because they're the ones most commonly used. However there are a few others including:

**SoftwareAG Adabas™**: A relational Database Manager, it also comes with a Transaction Manager. You can also access Adabas databases from CICS.

**CA-Datacom®**: A relational Database Manager. CA-Ideal™ is a Transaction Manager that is often used with CA-Datacom - or you can use CICS. CA-Datacom can also run on other platforms, and provides a service so that web applications can access the data (including SOAP access).

**CA-IDMS®** – Another relational Database Manager from CA.

## Do I Really Need to Buy This Stuff?

Do you really need to spend all that money on a Database and Transaction Manager? Well, no, not really. But if you don't, the chances are you're going to have to write programs that will do the same stuff – and that's very, very complicated. You'd have a lot of problems finding any computer site that doesn't have at least one Transaction Manager and one Database Manager, any many have a couple. They've decided that it's cheaper and easier to buy existing software. Because these products have been developed over years, they're way more robust and reliable than something written 'in-house'.

## The Last Word

Transaction and Database Managers are the heart of your Mainframe applications – managing databases, and the transactions accessing them. IMS, CICS and DB2 are by far the most common, but there are others that you can choose from.

# Chapter 6: Application Development on z/OS

Up to now, we've talked about the Mainframe hardware, the operating system, Transaction and Database Managers, and networks. So if you set up all of this, what you'll have is a Mainframe happily humming away in your computer room – and doing absolutely nothing for you. It's like a restaurant with no staff. The chefs are ready to cook, and all the tables, crockery and cutlery are ready. But there's no-one opening the restaurant or taking bookings. To get your Mainframe working for you, you need applications.

## What's an Application?

It's a group of programs (or application programs). Think of everything we've talked about so far as a blank canvas, with brushes and paint alongside. Everything is there, you just need to pick up the brush and create the Mona Lisa.

In fact Mainframes can pretty much do anything you want. Want to manage bank accounts and have internet banking? No problem. Want to computerize all your accounting? Can do. In either of these cases, get the Transaction and Database Managers you need and write the application to do it. Want to have the best graphical game on the planet? Choose another platform - Mainframes don't do graphics well.

Let's take a hypothetical bank - MakeMoney bank. They've bought a Mainframe, z/OS, and lots of other software. Now, they need an application to keep track of user bank accounts. Maybe one program to handle withdrawals, a second to handle deposits, and a third for account balance requests. All of these will run in an application environment and access databases through a Database Manager. They will be secured using your security software. But they will do what MakeMoney bank wants.

You can write your own application or buy one 'off the shelf.' You can also buy software like SAP, CSC Hogan™ or Oracle PeopleSoft™ that provide a lot of the features you're looking for, and gives you a way to 'finish it off' so it does exactly what you need.

## What's an Application Environment?

Think about an application program. Firstly, it needs to run somewhere - in some address space. Then, it's going to need to communicate with a user - get information from the user, send information to the user, and even find out who the user is (usually by a userid and password) for security. You could write your own programs to do this yourself, but this is a lot of work. A much better idea would be to use something that does this for you - an application environment.

An application environment can also provide a toolbox for things like accessing files or submitting batch jobs. We've already talked about how our Transaction Managers also provide an application environment. There are, however, other application environments that don't include a Transaction Manager – like TSO/E and batch. Some software products you buy may include their own application environment – like IBM NetView® or BMC CONTROL-M.

## How to Create an Application Program

When you write an application program, you'll be writing in a programming language. Languages can be either:

**Interpreted**: You write the program, and it's ready to go. When you run the program the application environment interprets each instruction and executes it. JCL, IBM REXX™, SAS® and CA–Easytrieve® are all interpreted.

**Compiled**: You write the program and put it through a program called a compiler to create *object code*. You then *bind* or *link-edit* this object code to create a *load module* (more on load modules in a second). IBM COBOL, PL/1, C and C++; Adabas Natural™; and SAS/C™ are all compiled. You'll also hear about Assembler (High Level Assembler or HLASM). You pass this language through an Assembler rather than a compiler, but this is really the same thing.

Java is a bit different – computer geeks will tell you that it's both compiled and interpreted. But you can think of it as being compiled. Java has one interesting difference - no binding or link-editing is required.

In general compiled programs are harder to get running, but are much faster. So let's look at a recipe for 'baking' a traditional compiled program:

## Recipe for Creating a COBOL Program

Serves One

Ingredients:

- 1 COBOL Compiler.
- 1 z/OS Operating System.
- 1 TSO/E Logon.
- 1 Application Environment (such as CICS, IMS or TSO).

Method:

- Logon to TSO/E, and use ISPF to get into an editor. Edit a dataset to create your source code (the instructions for your program) – designing it to run under your chosen application environment.
- Save the dataset holding your source code.
- Compile your source code to create an object module - use either online panels in ISPF or a batch job.

- Bind your object module with others to create a load module. Use the z/OS Binder from ISPF panels or a batch job.

- Setup your application environment to run your program.

- Run your program as often as you want.

All the traditional languages running on z/OS go through this path – but z/OS also handles new languages like Java and C - and these can run on z/OS UNIX. So today, you could use the UNIX shell to edit the program, invoke a compiler and run the Binder.

## *Binding Object Code*

You've seen from the recipe that compilers generally create object code. But you can't run object code; you need to create a *load module*. To do this you pass the object code through the Binder. The Binder (or Link-Editor as it used to be known) comes free with z/OS.

The binder brings together all the programs that will be in the load module and sets up how the load module will run. Let's take our COBOL program we've just baked. Let's say that this program (Program A) calls another program (Program B) to do some function. To call Program B from Program A you've got a couple of choices:

1. Write Program B as a separate program. This is slow because Program A must move the program in from disk every time it needs it.

2. Write Program B as a system program, meaning that it is always in memory and ready. This is faster but a lot harder to write and setup – and you can only have a limited number of system programs.

3. Include Program B in the load module. When Program A runs the entire load module is loaded from disk, including Program B. Most application programs use this option.

Many programs actually use option 3 without you knowing it. For example, if you write a program to run under CICS, the load module will include two CICS programs (one at the very front, one at the very back).

So the Binder puts all the object modules into a load module and also checks that all the modules you need are there.

## Pre-Compilers – Compiling Before You Compile

The recipe above works fine. However some application environments and Database Managers require you to pass your program through a *pre-compiler* before you compile it.

Pre-compilers convert system requests into your language, ready for your compiler. For example, the DB2 pre-compiler converts DB2 SQL requests into a form ready for use. This process includes creating another module that is used by DB2 called a *Database Request Module* (DBRM). CICS also has a pre-compiler that converts CICS requests.

# How to Develop an Application

We know what you're thinking: "You've already covered this. You write the program, compile it, and you're away." Well, not exactly. The actual coding is only a small part of the overall application development process. Here are some things that have to happen:

## 1. Decide on the Project Scope

Or in other words, figure out exactly what you want to do. This sounds trivial, but is actually very important. You don't want to spend up big for an application that doesn't do what you want it to do.

## 2. See if it is Feasible

Will it work at all? Do you have enough money to pay for it? Can you get all the resources you need to make it work? You'll have technical people, business people and Business Analysts looking at:

- **Where to run**. Should it run in IMS on z/OS, or Oracle on UNIX?

- **Custom or off-the-shelf.** Modify an existing application, buy something off-the-shelf, or develop something new?
- **Costs.** Manpower, software, and hardware. And we're not only talking about the cost of development, but also the ongoing costs of running and supporting the application.
- **Risk.** Is there a chance of affecting your existing systems?
- **Time to complete.** How long will it take to develop?

> **Your Three Application Environments**
>
> For any applications you have, you won't have one system running it; you'll almost certainly have three:
>
> - A **Test Environment** used by programmers and developers to test their programs as they write them.
> - A **Quality Assurance (QA)** environment where testers test changes made by programmers and developers. Many organizations have a 'test suite' – a set of standard tests that every change must pass before being eligible to move into Production.
>
>   The QA environment can also be called an **Acceptance**, or **User Acceptance Testing** (UAT) environment.
>
> - Your **Production** environment – this is where you do your real work.
>
> Any changes made to your applications are *migrated* from test to QA (when they're ready), and then from QA to Production (when they have passed all QA testing).
>
> By using this system, you're minimizing the chances of programming errors (or bugs) getting into your Production systems.

## 3. Get All the Resources You Need

You've decided to go ahead with the project. Now you need to get all the resources you need:

- Get and setup the hardware and software for development environments and any test systems.
- Get the personnel you need – programmers, testers, and support people.

- Do any research and training needed.

## 4. Design the Application

This is where you figure out the details of how you're going to create your application, like:

- What programs will need to be created.
- How these programs will work together.
- How these programs will fit into any existing applications.
- What transactions and databases will be needed.
- What changes need to be made to any existing applications, transactions and databases.
- How you're going to make sure that all these programs will do the job needed.

Mainframe applications can be very large, so you'll often have a 'high level' design, and then break this up into smaller pieces that different groups or programmers can do.

New development on Mainframe applications today often spans different application environments, making them *composite applications*. Programming to web enable legacy applications is a classic example of this.

## 5. Develop the Application

This is where your programmers write the programs that will make up the application. But they don't just write the programs. They'll test them in a test environment (*unit testing*), and even have them reviewed by another programmer (to check for any errors they may have missed).

Application development is usually broken up into pieces, making it possible for many programmers to code at the same time. There will be a lot of co-ordination so that a program written by one programmer works with a program written by another.

> ## Mainframe Software Support
>
> Mainframe software has the best support of any software on Earth – if you have a problem you can call a help desk to have it fixed (though the details will depend on your software agreement).
>
> When you report a problem with your software, most vendors have three layers of support:
>
> **Level 1**: Your first port of call. Level 1 will open a problem record so it can be tracked They will also search to see if the problem has happened before, and if not assign the problem to the right Level 2 team. Level 1 support usually doesn't know the details of your software or how to use it. Think of them as a switchboard.
>
> **Level 2**: These teams know your software. They're familiar with how it works, and the more common problems. They'll work with you to try and resolve your problem. If they can't, they'll pass the problem onto the right Level 3 team.
>
> **Level 3**: These are often (but not always) the team that actually develops the software. They can go through the software's source code, and figure out what's going wrong. Sometimes they may decide that there's a problem with the software, and will change the software. IBM in this case will open an APAR (Authorised Program Analysis Report), meaning a record to let everyone know that there is a request to make a change to the software.
>
> Level 3 (or sometimes a separate group called the *Change Team*) will fix the problem, and will send you the fix to install on your system. IBM calls this a Program Temporary Fix, or PTF. They may also try to think of a temporary solution to your problem to get you up and running as fast as possible while you wait for them to develop a PTF.

## *6. Test the Application*

This will generally be on a Quality Assurance environment – separate from both the test environment used by your programmers and any existing production. You'll have separate people testing the applications from those doing the development. These testers will look for problems, and when they find them (and they will), report them back to the developers to be fixed.

## 7. Prepare the Application for Production

There's a good chance that your application will need to work with existing applications. So you'll need to plan how you can 'cutover' your application to production without affecting your existing production systems.

You'll also need to do things like:

- Train users on how to use the new system.
- Plan how the application will be installed.
- Plan how the application can be backed out if it causes problems.
- Install any hardware and software needed for the application.
- Prepare operations plans for the new application: i.e. backups, Disaster Recovery plans, security and user support.

## 8. Cutover the Application to Production

At last you can now cut the application into production, and it's done - you're finished. Except that application development is rarely fully completed - people often talk about a *development cycle*. Once written the application will often need to be enhanced or changed, and this means starting again from the beginning.

OK, so the good news is that you've completed development, and your application is running in production. The bad news is that the work isn't over. Now you have to support it.

# Supporting an Existing Application

An existing application is like a car – you've bought the car and it works fine. But you're still going to have to service the car regularly, fix things when they go wrong, and teach your children to drive it when they're old enough. Applications aren't all that different.

## 1. Fix It When It Breaks

Applications are very complex things, and the chances are that there are bugs in the code – especially in new code. So when these bugs appear you're going to need a programmer to fix them, and migrate these fixes into production.

If your applications run 24 hours a day, you'll almost certainly have a 'Duty Programmer' on call. So if there's a problem at 3:00am, there's someone who can look at the problem and fix it.

> ### A Serviced Office for your Programs: Language Environment
>
> If you work in an office, you'll be provided with things like stationery, desks and lighting to help you do your job. For your application programs the *runtime environment* provides similar things. Things like:
>
> - **Someone to open up the office in the morning and collect the mail.** The runtime environment sets things up for your application program when it starts. It also gets data that is passed in to your program from the program that calls it.
>
> - **Pens, staplers and photocopiers.** The runtime environment provides functions that a program can call; things like date and time functions, services for running in different countries (with different languages), and mathematical functions (like square root).
>
> - **Cleaners.** If your program crashes, the runtime environment will clean things up. It may also produce a dump, and output messages to help you fix the error. It will also provide a facility where programmers themselves can decide what to do if their program crashes.
>
> - **Someone to lock up and turn off the lights when you leave.** The runtime environment cleans up after your program, and provides a way for it to pass things back to the program that called it.
>
> Today IBM's Mainframe languages (COBOL, PL/1, C, C++ and Fortran) have a common runtime environment. It's called *Language Environment*, and it comes free with z/OS.

## 2. Maintain It

Applications are almost never static. They regularly need to change, because:

- The business needs new or modified features. This can be as simple as a new report, or as complicated as a whole new set of features.

- Government regulations require changes.

- You need to change your code to work with new software. For example, you may need to change the code so it will work with a new version of z/OS or CICS.

- The application is too slow, and needs to be tuned. It's quite often that an application is written and then used far more than originally thought. So you need to make it faster or capable of handling larger workloads.

- Things occur that you haven't thought of. The Year 2000 problem was a classic example of this. Many organizations had to change their applications so they would work after the year 2000.

## 3. Support People Using It

It's easy to forget, but the most important thing about an application is the people using it – the bank tellers using a banking application, the accountants using a financial application. These people need support, and this means:

- A contact to help them with problems. This is usually a Help Desk. They will have people who will try to answer question and fix problems - and if they can't, they'll know someone who can.

- Someone to teach them how to use it. This is an ongoing process. Experienced people will move to a new job and new people will move in and need education. You'll also have to teach them any new functions you introduce.

- Someone to manage the security; i.e. who can do what. This is also an on-going job as people move in and out of positions.

- A way to tell them what's happening. If the application will be unavailable for a day for maintenance, you'll need a way to let the users know.

## Why Your Source Code is Important

It's very simple. If you don't have the source code, you can't support the application. You can't recompile the code, you can't make changes to it, and there's a good chance you won't be able to fix things when they go wrong. Losing an application's source code has to be one of the biggest nightmares for any Application Programming Manager.

So you need a Database Manager to hold your source code. There are a few on the market like:

- IBM SCLM.
- CA-Librarian®.
- CA-Panvalet®.

Some organizations may also choose to store their source code on a different platform – using software like IBM Rational ClearCase™.

This software not only stores your source code, but can also:

- Secure the source code. So only certain people can change it.
- Stop multiple people from changing the same program at the same time. So if one person has checked out a program to modify it, a second person can't also modify the program.
- Hold different versions. You can see the latest version of a program, and all the previous versions. This is useful for seeing what has changed, and even for backing out changes.
- Provide utilities to backup the source code databases.

- Enforce standards. A big example of this is the compiler options. This software can force programs to be compiled in a standard way. Similarly programming standards and change management standards can be enforced. We talk more about change management in Chapter 9.

- Recording who does what. So you can see who has updated a program.

- Track changes. Let's say that there a problem, and three programs need to be changed. The software links the three changes to a record – which records the problem, who changed it, and how it was changed.

# Why Is It So Hard To Develop Mainframe Applications?

Mainframe applications almost always take longer to develop than applications on other platforms. Why? Three reasons:

- **It's harder.** Developing applications using older languages like Assembler, COBOL and PL/1 is more difficult than newer languages like C and Java. Also, application programming under CICS and IMS is more difficult than under other application environments on other platforms.

- **They're often more important.** Because your Mainframe applications are usually the core of your business, there's less tolerance if they fail. So development will take longer (usually one person will write some code, and a second developer will check or review this code) and there will be more testing.

- **They're usually not new.** It's rare to develop a completely new application on the Mainframe. Normally you will change or enhance an existing application, or write an application that talks with an existing application. So before you can even think about writing anything new you need to understand how the existing application works, and what effect your changes will have on it. And as Mainframe applications have been developed over a lot of years, this can be quite complicated.

# Application Development Gadgets and Goodies

There are a lot of tools and support software that try to make your application programming work easier. Let's look at some.

## Development Environments

These are environments that make it easier to create applications programs. They may provide a nice interface for programmers, ways to enforce coding standards, a testing environment, and debugging tools. Some examples are:

- IBM Rational® Application Developer.
- ASG-Existing Systems Workbench™ (ESW®) Suite
- Serena™ StarTool® suite.
- IBM Websphere Developer for zSeries.

Some development environments give you a way to develop and test Mainframe applications on PCs (saving you the cost of setting up test environments on the Mainframe), such as:

- Micro Focus® Mainframe Express™.
- Tachyon® Assembler Workbench™.

## Change Management Tools

You have lots of code and lots of programmers. How can you keep track of what's changing and the possible effects if a change causes problems? Why was this change made? Are you sure that all the defects found in your code have been fixed?

Change management tools help you with this. Such tools help to track code changes, manage code versions and builds, and keep track of reported code defects. Examples include

- Serena ChangeMan® suite.

- CA Endevor® Software Change Manager.

## Debugging Tools

If you have a bug in your program, it can be hard to find out where the problem is. These tools help find those bugs:

- IBM Debug Tool for z/OS.
- IBM HLASM Toolkit.
- ASG-SmartScope™.

---

### How Many COBOLs Are There?

You'd expect that when different programmers talk about the COBOL programming language they're talking about the same thing. Well, they may not be...

The IBM COBOL compiler of choice is Enterprise COBOL for z/OS. However there are also some older IBM COBOL compilers:

- OS/VS COBOL.
- VS COBOL II.
- COBOL for OS/390.

The COBOL for OS/390 and VS COBOL II languages are very similar to Enterprise COBOL for z/OS. They run fine on z/OS providing they're using the Language Environment runtime libraries, and can generally be compiled by Enterprise COBOL without any code changes.

OS/VS COBOL programs are a bit different, and may need to be changed before they can be compiled using some of the newer compilers.

---

## Performance Tools

If your applications are too slow you need to look at their performance and determine what changes are needed to make them faster. This software gives you tools to do this, and can sometimes recommend changes:

- Macro 4 ExpeTune.

- ASG-SmartTune™.

## *Test Tools*

Testing an application isn't straightforward. You need to create *testcases* that comprehensively test all your application's functions. You then need to analyze the results of these tests (e.g. screen output, database contents, or file output). You may also need to *stress test* your application - see how the application performs under a production load (when it does as much work as it would when running in production). There are a lot of tools in all shapes and sizes that can help, including:

- ASG-SmartTest™.
- CA-InterTest® suite and CA-Verify®.
- IBM TPNS.

## The Last Word

Your applications make the Mainframe do what you want it to do – they're important. You'll be spending a lot of time, money and effort to develop and support them.

# Chapter 7: Accessorize - Software for the Mainframe

You can tell by the anguished screams from the office that the Mainframe Manager is new to z/OS. He's screaming because he's just seen a list of software running on his Mainframe – and how much it all costs. The average z/OS image runs a lot of software - 40 different packages on one z/OS image isn't unusual. But what does all of it do, and do you really need it?

We've already talked about a lot of this software; the different components of z/OS itself, language compilers, Application Development software, and Database and Transaction Managers. So let's have a look at some of the other things on the market.

But before we start, remember that we can't give you every single piece of software that's out there. What we can do is tell you some of the general categories. We'll also give examples of some of the more popular ones (but remember that we're not recommending any, and we're not getting any money or royalties for mentioning them).

## Monitoring Tools

Your z/OS system is doing a lot of work, and lots of different sorts of work. Monitors are programs that keep track of what's happening, and if there are any problems that need to be looked at. They're usually used in two ways:

- By technical people to find and fix problems. The monitors make it much easier to find out what the problems are and where they occur. Monitors can also provide advanced tracing features for further information about what's happening, and functions for historical analysis.

- As a 'nanny.' The monitor is setup by technical people so that it automatically detects problems, and can let the right people know - by email, an alert on a screen, or even an SMS on your mobile phone. As z/OS systems can be quite complicated, having a single pane of glass telling you if there are any problems can be very appealing.

So what sorts of monitors are there?

---

**The American Dream – Charles Wang and Computer Associates**

Most Mainframe sites will be familiar with software giant, Computer Associates (CA). From humble beginnings with their sorting package CA-Sort, CA is now the third largest software company on the planet. They sell more Mainframe software than any other software company outside of IBM. And most of these products have been 'inherited' from the acquisition of other software companies – over 50 of them.

The story of the man who formed CA is perhaps even more extraordinary. With just four years programming experience and a handful of software sales jobs, Charles Wang founded CA in 1976. A Chinese immigrant from Shanghai, he went from the streets of Queens in New York to become the CEO of a major global corporation.

Charles Wang left CA in August 2000.

---

## z/OS Monitors

These monitor the z/OS system itself. They can be used to see z/OS *internals* (what's happening inside z/OS), what's running, and how the system is performing. Some examples are:

- IBM Tivoli OMEGAMON® XE for z/OS.
- BMC MAINVIEW for z/OS.

- ASG-TMON® for z/OS™.

## IMS Monitors

If you have IMS the chances are that you'll have a monitor. IMS itself doesn't provide a lot of tools for problem determination or performance monitoring. Some IMS monitors are:

- IBM Tivoli OMEGAMON XE for IMS.
- BMC MAINVIEW for IMS.
- ASG-TMON® for IMS™.

## DB2 Monitors

DB2 monitors include:

- IBM DB2 Performance Expert.
- ASG-TMON® for DB2™.
- IBM Tivoli OMEGAMON XE for DB2.
- BMC MAINVIEW for DB2.

---

**Where Did The Third Party Vendors Go?**

A Third Party Vendor, or ISV (Independent Software Vendor), is someone that sells software for the mainframe and isn't IBM. There's a lot of this software, so it makes sense that there used to be lots of ISVs.

But over the past decade or two, the larger Mainframe software companies have been buying or merging with smaller ISVs – particularly IBM, Computer Associates and BMC. Today there are far less ISVs, but they're bigger.

This is also why some ISVs sell more than one product that does the same thing. For example CA has two security products: CA-Top Secret and CA-ACF2.

---

Chapter 7: Accessorize

## CICS Monitors

CICS monitors can monitor performance, provide extra tracing facilities, and tell you what's going on within a CICS region. Some are:

- IBM CICSPlex Systems Manager.
- IBM OMEGAMON XE for CICS.
- ASG-TMON® for CICS™.
- BMC MAINVIEW for CICS.

## Network Monitors

Your networks can get very complicated; so many sites have a monitor to look after them. These monitors can also be setup to automatically perform actions if a problem is found. Some examples include:

- IBM Tivoli NetView.
- CA NetMaster™.
- BMC MAINVIEW for Network Management.

## Other Monitors

You can find monitors for all sorts of things. For example:

**DASD Monitors**: These ease and automate the job of keeping track of disk space usage, free space, and disk performance. When you have thousands of disk devices, DASD monitors can become attractive. Examples include BMC DASD MANAGER PLUS™, Rocket® MAINSTAR® and IBM OMEGAMON XE for Storage.

**Compuware® STROBE**: This is really in a category of its own. A CAT scan for your programs, STROBE lets you analyze in detail an application's performance, and what it's doing.

**Database Access Performance Monitors:** BMC APPTune™ analyses the performance of SQL statements in an application accessing DB2.

***Composite Application Monitors:*** IBM Tivoli Composite Application Manager and BMC MAINVIEW TRANSACTION ANALYZER™ are products that help monitor applications that span multiple application environments and platforms.

## Monitors of Monitors

Yes, you can even buy software that monitors the monitoring software. This software generally works with other monitors, providing a single screen showing what's happening and what problems there are. This screen can be a Mainframe or Windows screen. Some examples are:

- BMC EVENT MANAGER™.
- IBM Tivoli Monitoring.
- CA Unicenter®.

Monitors are very handy, and in some cases essential. But what they provide comes at a price: they can be very CPU hungry.

The bottom line is that most sites will have some monitoring software to suite their needs and bank balance. This software allows technical people find and fix problems faster, and gives you early warning of a potential problem.

# Tape Management Software

In Chapter 2, we talked about tape libraries, and how much work it was to manage a library of thousands of tapes. Well, tape management software makes this job easy – almost all sites will have it. Some examples are:

- IBM DFSMSrmm™.
- BMC CONTROL-M/Tape™.
- CA-1®.

# Reporting Tools

With so much data stored in your databases, you want to be able to access information from them. To write a dedicated application to do this takes time and money. And invariably these reports change alongside business requirements.

So software vendors have developed *reporting languages* that give you an easy way to create reports from your data. They're quick to develop, and can access data in most databases. Some examples are:

- CA Easytrieve®.
- SAS®.

# Output Management Software

By output we mean reports and output from jobs and started tasks. A typical site will have a lot of these (thousands every day isn't unusual). For each one, the question is:

- How long do we keep it?
- Who do we let view, print or delete it (security)?
- How many copies do we print out, and who needs to receive them?

Output management software helps with this. They generally provide a way for users to view the report, a security mechanism to control access to the report (or to a portion of it), and a way to automate printing and addressing of reports. They can also include an archiving feature. Some examples include:

- BMC Control-D™
- IBM RMDS.
- CA View®.

## Software for a Disaster

Ideally, disasters don't happen. You have backups, rigid change management procedures, and a backup plan if these fail. But if these aren't enough or you want extra peace of mind, the following packages are for you:

- **BMC Recovery Manager™**: A suite of products that speed up the recovery of your databases.

- **Compuware AbendAid™ & IBM Fault Analyzer**: These two products assist Applications Programmers in debugging application crashes.

- **IBM DFSMShsm & Innovation ABR**: This software can automate the backup and restoration of critical files.

- **EMC® Catalog Solution® & IBM ICFRU**: These let your Systems Programmers recover catalogs. Catalogs are files that remember which disk drive your files are on; when you have over 100 disk drives this becomes important. Without catalogs your z/OS system simply doesn't run.

## Performance Software

Software that can make things run faster:

- **BMC MAINVIEW Batch Optimizer™**: Makes your batch jobs run faster without code changes.

- **IBM CICS Online Transmission Time Optimizer for z/OS**: Optimizes data sent by CICS programs to 3270 terminals without code changes.

- **BMC Energizer for CICS**: Improves the performance of your CICS regions.

# Decision Support Software

This is software to process all that SMF information we've talked about before. This SMF data includes a wealth of performance, security and accounting information. Decision support software helps you process this information, getting meaningful reports and information:

- CA-MICS® Resource Management.
- IBM Tivoli Decision Support (TDS).
- Merrill Consultants MXG.

# File Transfer Software

With TCP/IP, moving files between the Mainframe and other computing platforms is easy. But TCP/IP is relatively new to the Mainframe – before this you needed other software to help:

- Barr/RJE.
- Sterling Commerce Connect:Direct™.

# Printing Software

We've already talked in the z/OS section about printing from z/OS. But there are some other tools to help you:

- **IBM Document Composition Facility (DCF):** A way of formatting documents on the Mainframe ready for printing on Enterprise printers.
- **InfoPrint Page Printing Formatting Aid:** For formatting files for printing on Enterprise printers without changing code.
- **InfoPrint XML Extender for z/OS:** Translate XML (Extended Markup Language) into a format for Enterprise printers.

## Other Goodies on the Market

There are all sorts of software on the market. Here's just a taste:

- **Nexus MEMO:** Formerly known as Verimation MEMO, this is an email package for the Mainframe.

- **Beta Systems Harbor™ & Innovation FDR/Upstream®:** Backup and restore data from other platforms (such as Windows and UNIX) to your Mainframe tape drives.

- **IBM BookManager**: A library on your Mainframe.

- **Compuware FileAID™, IBM File Manager, and Serena StarToolFDM:** These three packages let you browse and edit any sort of Mainframe file or database.

- **IBM Tivoli InfoMan:** Information management software that is often used for problem and asset management.

- **Chicago-Soft Quick-Ref™:** A quick reference for z/OS. Look up messages, commands, language syntax and other handy things without going to z/OS manuals.

## The Last Word

Like any other popular computing system, there's a whole lot of software you can buy for the Mainframe. What you'll have will depend on your needs and budget.

# Chapter 8: What Do All These People *DO*? People You Need to Run a Mainframe

Get all your Mainframe people together in one room, and that room will need to be a lot larger than you think. New Mainframe Managers are often amazed at the number of people they're paying to run their Mainframe. There are three main reasons for this:

- Mainframes are harder to run than other computing systems.
- Mainframes are usually more important to the organization – so there's more care needed in running them.
- Mainframes often do more work than other computing systems.

So who are all these people? Let's meet them.

## Operators

Its 4am in the computer room and a few badly dressed people lounge in chairs facing a bank of computer screens. There's a TV running in the background and a half eaten pizza lies on a table nearby. This is a common (and usually incorrect) perception of your computer Operators. But your Operators are important – they're the guardians of your Mainframe.

Mainframe sites usually have Operators onsite 24 hours a day, seven days a week. There will usually be one group, or *shift*, of Operators working at any one time.

## What They Do

- **Watch over your Mainframe and Network:** If there's a problem with the Mainframe, like a hardware failure or application crash, your Operators are there to quickly detect the problem and start the process to fix it.

- **Startup and Shutdown the Mainframe and Applications:** For example, you may have one IMS region that only runs during business hours, or you need to shutdown z/OS to do some periodic maintenance.

- **Mount Tapes:** Although most sites have an Automated Tape Library, sometimes you need a tape that's outside the library to be mounted.

- **Manage Tapes:** We've already talked about tape management in Chapter 2. Operators manage offsite and external tapes. They also periodically clean your tape drives, and schedule the replacement of older tapes.

- **Manage Printer Output:** Sites with an enterprise printer will need someone to :
    o Make sure there's paper for the printer.
    o Load any special forms for special print runs (like a bank's account statements on a special form with their letterhead).
    o Send the printout to where it needs to go.

- **Monitor your Batch:** Operators will monitor your batch runs, including your important overnight batch. If there's a problem, they will try to fix it (if it's a small problem), or call support. This is often especially important for your overnight batch.

- **Handle Queries:** People are often calling Operators to ask questions like: "who's the systems administrator on-call?", "has the batch run completed?", or "why isn't my job running?"

- **Perform Tasks for Other Support People:** For example, your Database Administrators may ask the Operators to shutdown DB2, run a few jobs that have already been prepared, and then restart DB2 at 2am. Similarly some sites have a change management procedure whereby Operators will actually perform the tasks necessary to make a change.

- **Liaise with Hardware Support Engineers:** You hardware will regularly need repair or maintenance. You need someone to liaise with the hardware engineers while they're onsite.

- **Monitor Other Computer Systems:** Mainframe Operators often also monitor other non-Mainframe computer systems.

- **Other things:** Some sites may allow Operators to do basic security administration, operate a help desk outside of business hours, and possibly even provide a 24 hour telephone switchboard. It's sometimes very handy to have someone there 24 hours a day.

## How They Get There

There's not a lot of formal training for Operators. Most Operators learn on-the-job, with supplementary learning in courses. Each shift will normally have a shift leader who is an experienced Operator, and he'll be teaching the more junior Operators how to do things. Some sites will also get other people like Systems Programmers and Database Administrators to give training to their Operators.

## The Last Word

The job of an Operator has changed over the years. With sites now using automated operation and automated job scheduling software, the number of Operators you need has reduced. Some sites even run a *lights out* Mainframe, meaning that no Operators work at night - everything is done by automated operations software. However the scope of an Operator's job has increased; they do a lot of work that was once the job of an Operations Analyst (more on them in a second), and even perform tasks on non-Mainframe computer systems.

> ### Share - Mainframe School?
> There aren't many computing user groups that have been around for more than 50 years. In fact there's just one: Share.
>
> An independent self-funded user group, Share concentrates on IBM computers – from management to technical issues. And although IBM features heavily, other vendors also get involved.
>
> Share's yearly conference is THE event for users of IBM computers. Vendors tell about what's new, and there are lots of information sessions: from learning zSeries Assembler to future direction of IMS. Possibly one of the best mainframe schools you can find. http://www.share.org

# Operations Analysts

It's easy to forget about Operations Analysts - they do the 'forgotten work.'

## *What They Do*

- **Manage Automated Operations**: Automated operations software has made the life of an Operator a lot easier. However to do this, someone has to setup and maintain all the automated operations rules, like:
    - What time things happen.
    - What to do when a certain event happens (like when z/OS starts up, or a program crashes).
    - How to determine the important problems from the less important ones.
- **Create and Manage Job Schedules:** Although Operators monitor the job schedules as they're running, the Operations Analyst actually creates the job schedule – including the coding

of a lot of the JCL. This involves a lot of work setting up automated batch scheduling software.

- **DASD Management:** This involves:
    - Organizing backups of disks and datasets.
    - Regularly defragmenting disks (consolidating free space).
    - Monitoring disk usage, and letting people know when disk space is getting low.
- **Help Operators:** Operations Analysts provide a lot of backup for the Operators. They help them fix problems (maybe a complicated batch job problem), setup systems and procedures (like what to do when there's an application failure), and even provide training.

## How They Get There

Many Operations Analysts start life as an Operator, and go from there. Again, there's a lot of on-the-job training from senior Operations Analysts and other technical people, supplemented by formal courses.

## The Last Word

Like Operators, the job of an Operations Analyst has changed over the years. While automated operations software has eased the job of an Operator, it's increased the technical workload of Operations Analysts. Operations Analysts also do more DASD management and technical JCL writing than before. They may even maintain some TSO/ISPF applications.

It's easy to forget all about Operations Analysts – their job isn't very visible. But like Operators, they're very important to your Mainframe environment.

# Security Administrators

With smaller computing platforms the Systems Administrator does all the security administration. But Mainframes can have thousands of users in different geographical areas. So the chances are that you'll have a security administration team that does this for you.

## What They Do

- Create logons for new users.
- Remove logons, security rules and datasets for users that no longer access the Mainframe.
- Reset passwords – when users forget them.
- Administer rules – who can access what.
- Other security administration work, such as monitoring security failures and performing security audits.

## How They Get There

Like Operators, Security Administrators get most of their training on the job, supplemented by some formal training.

## The Last Word

Because of the scale of Mainframes, many sites will have a security administration presence in each major team. So if an application programmer forgets their password, there's a local part-time administrator that can help. This part-time administrator is supported by the central security administration team.

Because your Mainframe security is so important, your Security Administrators are also very important.

# Application Developers

We've talked in our Applications chapter about the job of developing and supporting applications. Now the chances are that your Application Developers will comfortably outnumber your operations staff. This shows how difficult a task this is.

## What They Do

- Design and develop new applications.
- Support existing applications.

## How They Get There

Application Developers will usually have some programming qualification. This gives them the basic knowledge of how to program, which is supplemented by on-the-job training and formal courses.

## The Last Word

It's surprising how much work is involved not only in developing new applications, but supporting existing ones. In fact the chances are that you'll have a duty Applications Programmer who will get called at any time of day or night if an application fails.

# Application Testers

In our Applications chapter, we talked about how a separate group would test application program changes in a separate Quality Assurance environment. This is the role of Application Testers.

## What They Do

- Develop test cases to test applications.
- Run test cases, and check results.
- Document any problems found, and help Application Programmers understand what those problems are.

## How They Get There

There's no formal training to be a tester. Most of their training is on-the-job.

## The Last Word

It's easy to ask "Why do I need a tester – why can't I trust my Applications Programmers?" The fact is that all programmers make mistakes. They will find and fix most of them before the programs go to the testers, but testers will always find more. And the cost of a mistake making it into your production environment can be far higher than the cost of your test team.

---

### The Shrinking Need for Mainframe People

A Mainframe site today needs a lot less people than they would have 10 or more years ago. This is because:

- There's software that can do some of the job – like automated operations and automated job scheduling software.
- Mainframes are becoming easier to install and maintain.
- Some applications have moved to other platforms.
- Some organizations have centralized Mainframe operations to a single site, or moved the Mainframe operations to an external outsourcing company.

These developments mean that you need less mainframe technical people – but it certainly doesn't replace them altogether.

---

# Database Administrators

By now you've heard us saying this a lot: your data is critical. If you lose it or can't guarantee that it's correct, you're in trouble. Sounds like a job for a Database Administrator.

## What They Do

- Design and create databases, and change them when necessary.
- Organize regular backups and re-organizations of your databases and database logs.
- Monitor database and Database Manager performance, making improvements as needed.

- Manage the disks that your databases are on, so you don't get a database failure due to lack of disk space.

- Monitor database size – and possibly split databases if they become too big.

- Advise Application Programmers how they can create applications that access databases better.

- Investigate and fix any database related problems.

## How They Get There

Database Administrators are often (but not always) graduates. They will get a lot of training on-the-job, supplemented by formal courses and conferences (like Share). You also see Application Programmers and sometimes Operations Analysts become Database Administrators.

## The Last Word

Database Administrators actually do a lot of work that's invisible. But no-one knows your data and databases better.

# Systems Programmers

Your Systems Programmers know your Mainframe better than anyone else – and that's because they set it up.

## What They Do

They're your Systems Administrators. There are actually different types of Systems Programmers. In larger sites these Systems Programmers will be in separate teams. However smaller sites will possibly have Systems Programmers doing more than one of these tasks.

### z/OS Systems Programmers

- Install and customize the operating system and other systems software on the Mainframe.

- Install software updates and upgrades.

- Write exits and routines to assist in maintaining the operating system.
- Monitor systems performance and fix performance problems if they occur.
- Perform capacity management (more on this in the next chapter).
- Together with the Operations Analysts, perform DASD management tasks.
- Setup the security software and advise Security Administrators.
- Investigate and fix any systems related problems.
- Possibly develop applications for other groups – such as TSO/ISPF applications for Security Administrators, Database Administrators, and Operators.

With the introduction of UNIX System Services in z/OS, Systems Programmers have also become UNIX administrators.

## CICS Systems Programmers

- Install and customize CICS and other related systems software.
- Monitor CICS performance, and make changes if necessary.
- Investigate and fix any CICS related problems.
- Advise CICS Applications Programmers on CICS technical issues.

## IMS Systems Programmers

IMS Systems Programmers mainly deal with IMS Transaction Manager (TM). The IMS Database Administrator looks after the IMS Database Manager (DB). They:

- Install and customize IMS and other related systems software.
- Monitor IMS TM performance, and make changes if necessary.
- Investigate and fix any IMS TM related problems.

- Advise IMS Applications Programmers on IMS TM technical issues.
- Liaise with IMS DBAs in managing IMS DB.

> **The Shortage of Mainframe People**
>
> Mainframes are not sexy. They're old, different from other computing platforms, and don't really get a mention in University courses or the media. So it's no wonder that most computing graduates aren't interested in a Mainframe career.
>
> And even if they are, it takes a lot longer to train up a new graduate – for example around three years for a Systems Programmer. So today the number of Mainframe technical people is decreasing, and their average age increasing.
>
> Many people believe that this is becoming a crisis. Mainframes are actually doing more work, yet large numbers of senior technical people are reaching retirement age.

## Network Systems Programmers

Your network Systems Programmer manages SNA and TCP/IP networks. They:

- Design the SNA and TCP/IP network for the Mainframe.
- Customize VTAM and TCP/IP to implement the network design.
- Investigate and fix any network related problems.
- Monitor network performance, and fix any problems.
- Look after Communications Controllers.
- Look after other network related software and network performance monitors.

Networks can be the hardest things to maintain. Network Systems Programmers are rarely bored – and are often the first place people come when there's any problem even remotely relating to networks.

## How They Get There

There are two main types of Systems Programmers

- Those who have moved from operations (like Operations Analysts).
- University graduates.

Both still need a lot of training from formal courses and conventions (like Share), and on-the-job training.

## The Last Word

A major part of your Systems Programmer's job is to maintain supported hardware and software. This means that Systems Programmers always seem to be involved in a project to upgrade your hardware or systems software.

Systems Programmers are often the most under-used resource in a Mainframe site. They know more about Mainframe technology, and your Mainframe in particular, than anyone else.

# Other People

## Business Analysts

Your business people understand your business, and your Application Programmers understand how to create programs. But there's often a large gap between them. That's where a Business Analyst will come in. He's your bridge between the two, allowing your Applications Programmers to create programs that satisfy your business needs.

## Help Desk People

When computer users have a problem, they need someone to call and help them - a help desk. Your help desk people will have some knowledge about Mainframes and how they work, but often they won't be able to fix the problem. But they will know who in your organization can.

## Hardware People

Your Mainframe site has a lot of hardware: processors, disk, networks, tape drives and printers. These all need to be in a computer room, so someone has to manage the computer room environmentals (air conditioning, power, physical security, etc.). You also need someone to look after your backup generator, which is a complicated job in its own right. And there's the data cabling in the computer room, UPS, and even a raised floor to think of.

Some of this work may be done by external contractors or your operations people, but the chances are that you've got at least one person who has overall responsibility for all of this.

## Disaster Recovery Coordinator

With a critical computing system, you want a plan in case things go wrong – a Disaster Recovery Plan. For Mainframes these plans can be quite complicated, involving many different groups. So there's a good chance that you have a Disaster Recovery Coordinator to:

- Liaise with all groups necessary to create and maintain your Disaster Recovery plans.
- Organize regular Disaster Recovery tests.

## Trainers

You have a large Mainframe with many applications running on it. So your users need training; how to use the applications, how to logon to the Mainframe, and how to do their job. You'll probably have one or more people who will conduct this training.

## Your Fifth Column

Mainframe managers have a secret army that they may not even know exists – their 'Fifth Column.' In every group that uses a Mainframe – be it an end-user group (like a bank branch) or a technical group (like your Applications Programmers), there will often be one 'expert.' This is the person who's been there for a while and can answer questions and fix problems. People will usually approach this person before ringing your help desk or Mainframe technical people. These people are like gold to your organization.

## The Last Word

In many ways, your Mainframe technical people will be better trained than similar people on other platforms. This is because Mainframes are harder to maintain and they're more important to your business. And because of the importance of your Mainframe, failures are far less tolerated. This often means that your Mainframe people are more disciplined; they have stronger, better documented standards and procedures, and more rigid change management.

As Mainframes have developed the number of Mainframe people needed has been decreasing. But this is fortunate, as it's getting harder to find experienced Mainframe technical people. But however hard it is, you can't run a Mainframe without them.

# Chapter 9: Mainframe Manager Nightmares

We've been saying it all through this book, but Mainframe computers are different from the others:

- They use different technology (hardware and software).
- They have more users (sometimes thousands) working at any one time.
- They have more separate applications running.
- They do more work.
- They're critical to the business.

So if you've got a Mainframe, there are some unique issues that you need to think about. Let's have a look at some.

## What Do You Mean It's Unavailable?

When your entire business relies on your Mainframe, you don't want it to die on you – ever. The good news is that Mainframes have been staying alive for years. At times they have been a victim of their own success – it's easy to forget about your Mainframe when it quietly works in the background with no real problems. However keeping this Mainframe working with no downtime doesn't happen by magic – it needs to be well managed.

Organizations have developed ways to minimize the chance of a Mainframe failure. These include:

1. Controlling Changes.

2. Doing Things More Carefully.
3. Testing Everything.
4. Having a Plan B.

Let's have a look at these.

## 1. Controlling Changes

One of the major causes of computer failures is change. For example:

- The installation of some new equipment (that doesn't work).
- A software upgrade (that fails).
- An application program change (that introduces a bug).

So to minimize the risk of these changes you'll almost certainly have a rigid procedure to be followed before anything can change - a *change management* procedure. This procedure will vary from organization to organization, but will often look something like this:

1. All changes have to be submitted to a manager or committee for review. The person wanting the change will need to document things like:

- What the change is (*"I'm adding new function X to Internet Banking"*).
- What is affected by the change (*"The Internet Banking system"*).
- What will be affected if the change fails (*"The entire Internet Banking system"*).
- The risk of the change (*"low risk – change has been running in our test systems for two months, and has gone through quality assurance"*).
- How the change will be implemented – including what needs to happen before and after the change (*"Operators will shutdown Internet Banking, run the batch job I have prepared, and restart Internet Banking"*).
- Any outage that will happen during the change (*"Internet Banking will be down for 30 minutes to allow the change to be implemented"*).

- How the change can be backed out if it fails (*"Operators will shutdown Internet Banking, run a second batch job I have prepared to backout the change, and restart Internet Banking"*).

- When the change will occur (*"January 28th at 03:30"*).

- Who checked their change to make sure it won't fail *("The Application Programming Manager")*.

2. The Change Manager or committee will review all changes for approval or rejection. They will also check that changes occurring at the same time don't clash with each other.

3. If the change is approved, it can be done.

4. Support people will be given a list of all the changes. If there's a problem, they can look to see if a recent change could have caused this problem.

## 2. Doing Things More Carefully

It's so easy for someone to make a mistake – press the wrong key, do something on the wrong machine, unplug the wrong cable. But when your computer systems are critical, you want everyone to do things more carefully. Here are some examples of how organizations achieve this:

- Mainframe computer personnel have rules or procedure that they follow to do their job. For example:
    - Operators will usually follow documented step by step instructions when doing many high risk tasks, such as restarting z/OS.
    - Systems Programmers will usually follow standard procedures when changing anything: how the change is to be made, a standard way to backout the change, how to test it, and who needs to check it.
- If something has to be done to the production system it will be done at a time when systems will be least affected if the change fails. So if a Systems Programmer has to make a change, he will

try and wait for a time when any impact of the change failing is minimized.

- Technical people with a logon ID that lets them make changes to a production environment will have a second logon ID that doesn't. They'll use this second ID for their day to day work and that first ID only when production changes are needed. This minimizes the chance of them accidentally changing something in the production environment.

- Many organizations will implement a change freeze during periods when it is especially important to have their Mainframes working (like Christmas or the end of the financial year). During this time, *nothing* changes.

So to put it simply, Mainframe technical people will often take more care than technical people on other computing systems.

## 3. Testing Everything

Everything on a Mainframe is tested - everything. Nothing goes into your production environment without being fully tested in your test or quality assurance environment. If some hardware changes, you will allow enough time in your change window to test that hardware, and backout the change if there's a problem.

## 4. Having a Plan B

What if, despite all of your plans and procedures, something still goes wrong? You need to have a plan ready - a Plan B. For example:

- Technical people (like Systems Programmers and Application Programmers) will be on-call 24 hours a day, seven days a week. So if a problem appears, it can be fixed regardless of the day or time.

- Operators will have a list of people they can call if something goes wrong: from Database Administrators to managers, electricians, and even Security Administrators.

- There will be a Disaster Recovery Plan (more on this soon).

# Where Does All the Money Go?

By now you know that Mainframes cost more than other computing platforms. There is the cost of:

- Buying the hardware and software.
- Support and maintenance of the hardware.
- Support and licensing of the software.
- Environmentals (air conditioning, computer room, electricity, Uninterruptible Power Supplies, backup generators – the list can seem endless).
- People.
- Communications and networking infrastructure.
- Disaster Recovery infrastructure.
- Consumables (like printer paper and tape drive cleaning kits).

People often talk about the Total Cost of Ownership (TCO) - calculating the complete costs, not just the obvious ones. Mainframe managers are caught in the middle of two needs – to spend money to properly run and maintain the Mainframe, and to cut costs.

# Who's Paying for All of This?

Because of the size and cost of Mainframes, they're usually shared by different departments, groups, or even companies. These groups could share an entire Mainframe (with an LPAR each), a z/OS image, a CICS region, or even a single application.

If you're managing a Mainframe you need get enough money from your customers to cover your costs. So you'll probably be sending out regular invoices or bills to the users of your Mainframe. People call this *chargeout* or *chargeback*.

> ### Mainframe Software Costs - Pay for What You Use
>
> After buying Mainframe software you'll usually pay a regular licensing or maintenance fee that gives you the right to use the software, and support in case of a problem.
>
> For most software, IBM and other software vendors charge a fee that depends on the size of your processor. The larger the processor (or the higher the Millions of Service Units, or MSU rating), the more money you pay. This becomes a big issue if you decide to upgrade your processor.
>
> But recently, IBM and other software vendors have given customers another option: *sub-capacity pricing*. With sub-capacity pricing the cost of the software depends on the actual processor usage, not the size. So you can upgrade your processor, but only pay more money if you actually use more of the processor.

So you need a way of sharing the Mainframe costs fairly - but how? Firstly, you need a way of determining exactly how much work a user has done. And we have some good news: z/OS has the best resource monitoring using SMF and RMF or CMF. So for every user you can find out things like:

- CPU, memory, disk and tape space usage.
- Network usage.
- Amount of printing done.
- Number of batch jobs submitted.
- Number of transactions done.

So now all you need to do is decide a method of calculating your users' costs - and then get them to agree!

Many large sites have quite sophisticated systems that decide how much everyone needs to pay, and even automatically prepare regular invoices. However you can be sure that each user wants to pay as little as possible for their Mainframe share. So they'll be looking very carefully at every invoice they get.

> ### Hercules - A Mainframe on Your PC
> In 1999, Robert Bowler had some spare time. So he wrote a program that allowed a PC to emulate a zSeries mainframe. He called it Hercules.
>
> Today Hercules is Open Source software that runs under Linux, Windows and MacOS. Despite receiving no official support from IBM, Hercules is surprisingly popular. New releases are regularly produced to emulate the latest zSeries innovations from IBM.
>
> Hercules works with the latest operating systems that run on the zSeries including z/OS, z/Linux and z/VM. However it doesn't include these operating systems - users need to obtain them (and a license from IBM to run them). http://www.hercules-390.org

# Software and Hardware Support

Because Mainframes have been around for years, sites often rely heavily on some older pieces of hardware and software. But suppose one day you get an email from the manufacturer or vendor telling you they're going to stop support? This means that if something goes wrong with the hardware or software, there's no-one you can turn to for help. You're going to be relying on something that you may not be able to fix if it breaks. Let's look at two examples:

## IBM OS/VS COBOL

Many years ago if you wrote a COBOL program in z/OS, you compiled it using the IBM OS/VS COBOL compiler. Today OS/VS COBOL is no longer supported by IBM. IBM didn't just stop support - they notified users many years beforehand. They also gave users a migration path: migrate to the newer VS COBOL II compiler. The problem was that users needed to modify their old COBOL code to compile on the newer COBOL compiler, and to recompile everything.

## IBM Communications Controller

IBM has stated that it will discontinue supporting the 3745 and 3746 Communications Controllers in the next few years. However many organizations still rely on this hardware to run their production SNA networks. They've been quietly running without problems for years.

So all Communications Controller users now have to migrate their networks to a TCP/IP based network, or install IBM's new Communication Controller for Linux.

It's unreasonable to expect manufacturers and vendors to support everything they've sold forever. So Mainframe users that want their systems supported (and there aren't many who don't) will be upgrading them on a regular basis.

Take for example z/OS itself. IBM produces a new release of z/OS every year, and only supports the latest three z/OS releases. This means that z/OS users must upgrade their z/OS operating system at least once every three years. However upgrading an operating system is a lot of work. In fact, upgrading systems software is a large part of a Systems Programmer's job.

## Being Ready for a Disaster

Imagine one of these things happening to your Mainframe:

- Your entire basement computer room is flooded during a storm, destroying everything (including your tape library).

- An electrician performing maintenance on your UPS makes a mistake, and black smoke starts coming out of your networking equipment.

- A disk holding a critical database fails, and you can't use the last database backup (someone spilt coffee all over it).

What would happen to your business? A lot of organizations would be in serious trouble, and some may be unable to continue to operate. So it makes sense to have plans for these circumstances – Disaster Recovery Plans. They'll include things like:

**Backups:** Additional copies of critical data and systems disks will be kept so they can be recovered quickly. A copy of these backups will almost certainly be stored in another location (offsite) in case the entire building is destroyed.

**Disaster Recovery Site**: If a computing site is completely destroyed, the Mainframe processing needs to be done somewhere else. Many organizations keep another site ready in case this happens - a Disaster Recovery site. This site will be either:

- **Hot**: There's computing hardware at the site ready to use. If the entire building is destroyed, backups from an offsite location are moved to the Disaster Recovery Site, and restored on the hardware that is there waiting.

- **Cold**: There's no hardware waiting. So if the building is destroyed, new hardware must be found and installed before any restoring from backups can be done.

**Remote Copy**: This is where the hot Disaster Recovery site is actually running an image of the production site. The Disaster Recovery site is connected to the production site, and any updates to the production data are *mirrored* at the Disaster Recovery site. This way, the Disaster Recovery site can be up and running almost immediately after any failure.

**Duplicate Equipment:** There may be a spare set of hardware (like that network hardware with smoke pouring out of it) onsite.

If your Mainframe site is going to have Disaster Recovery Plans, you'll need to:

- Create them.

- Maintain them. Computer systems are always changing, so your plans need to be constantly reviewed and changed if necessary.

- Test them on a regular basis – you need to know if they really work.

# Mainframe People – Where Do I Get One?

We've talked in the previous chapter about how Mainframe people take longer to train, and can be harder to find than technical people on other platforms. Enough said.

# Paying Someone Else to Do It

Over the past decade or two, a lot of Mainframe users have decided that it's too hard to run a Mainframe. So they've gone and paid someone else to do it for them - an outsourcer or computing bureau. And the arguments for this are persuasive:

- The outsourcing company can often do it cheaper because of the economy of scale. They can share people, environmentals and hardware between clients.

- You don't have the complexities of looking after a Mainframe. You get to concentrate on your core business.

But there can be catches as well:

- You trust your core computing system and data to an external company.

- Once you give your Mainframe to an outsourcer, you lose all of your Mainframe people. It's going to be hard to get them all back again if you change your mind.

- Companies often don't realize all the work that their Mainframe department does – and the outsourcer may well charge more for this extra work.

Of course, it's not an all-or-nothing decision. You could decide to outsource only the printing of your statements (so you don't need an enterprise printer), or to pay someone just to manage your network for you.

There's certainly no right or wrong answer to the question "to outsource, or not to outsource." Every individual company will need to weigh up the advantages and disadvantages themselves.

## Why Is It Taking So Long?

It's a question that every help desk receives almost daily: "Why is my transaction/application/session working so slowly?" And it can be a difficult question to answer. It could be a problem with the:

- Mainframe operating system.
- Application environment (IMS, CICS, Websphere AS).
- Application.
- DASD or files.
- Network
- Computer that the user is working on (not the Mainframe).

Remember that there are a lot of people working on the Mainframe - so who do you talk to? Composite applications can make this problem even more difficult to solve.

But think about this: how long is too slow? One second? Two seconds? It's a hard question to answer. You may very well have a Service Level Agreement (SLA) with your clients that states how quickly a transaction should complete.

Mainframe performance problems often land first on a Systems Programmer's desk – they have the knowledge and the tools to measure transaction performance. And if nothing else, they can eliminate areas that can be the problem. But you'd be amazed at how much effort it can take to track down some of these performance problems.

# When Do We Get a New One?

If you remember, right at the beginning of the book we said that the amount of Mainframe processing around the world is increasing. If your organization follows this trend, then eventually your hardware won't be big enough. And we're not just talking about your processor. You could run out of:

- Disk space.
- Space in your Automated Tape Library.
- Capacity on your printer.
- Network capacity.

Well, the answer's obvious isn't it? Go buy more hardware or a bigger Mainframe! But there are some things to think about first:

- Mainframe hardware isn't cheap.
- With a bigger Mainframe processor, you'll probably have to pay more for your software licensing.
- You may need more room in your machine room for the new hardware.
- You may have to think about environmentals. Can your power supply handle more load? Can your air conditioning handle it?
- To install and migrate to this new hardware, you may need a large change window. When can you schedule this window?
- You may need to change some of your software or applications so they will work on the new equipment.
- Do you also need to upgrade hardware at your Disaster Recovery site?

So the bottom line is that you need to keep track of how busy or full your hardware is, and plan ahead for any hardware upgrades. This is called *capacity planning* or *capacity management*. Someone like a Systems Programmer will measure things like:

- Processor usage.
- Disk space usage.
- Tape usage.
- Network usage.

From this, you can start planning future upgrades, or possibly avoid them altogether by doing some things differently (like cleaning up old disk files, or changing applications so they use less processing power).

And this can also work if your Mainframe workload is decreasing. With good capacity management you can schedule downgrades to smaller processors and smaller disk subsystems – saving you money.

## Providing the Mainframe With a Good Home

It can seem like there's constantly people walking in and out of your computer room. Electricians, air-conditioning repairman, hardware technicians – what are they all doing?

Maintaining environmentals for a Mainframe (or any critical computer system) is a never-ending task. Your backup generator needs to be started and maintained regularly. It seems you're always got an air-conditioning technician trying to fix a hot spot in a corner of your computer room. And there's always new cabling that needs to be done.

It's all part of the fun of running a Mainframe.

## Keeping it Safe

If you want to give a Mainframe manager a reason for a nightmare – try a security breach. Now, we're not just talking about computer security and logons. We're also talking about:

- **Computer Room Security**: Not only do you need to protect your Mainframe, you also have a z/OS console in your computer room. Anyone with the knowledge can do a lot of damage with that z/OS console.

- **Tape Security:** Your backups hold confidential information so you will want to secure your tapes – including tapes sent offsite. You may also want to encrypt your tapes.

- **Network Security**: So people can't tap into your network to see sensitive information.

- **Printout Security:** If you produce paper reports that are sensitive, they need to be secured.

## The Last Word

We've talked a lot about some issues that non-Mainframe people may not have thought about. Most of these issues relate to the fact that Mainframes do more work, have been around longer, and process sensitive information which is critical to your organization.

# Chapter 10: The Last Word

When I was 21, I'd just finished a Computer Systems Engineering degree and I thought I was pretty clever. In four years I'd programmed in a couple of different Assembler languages, designed cards to slot into computers, and even designed my own silicon chip! I was hot.

And then I saw my first Mainframe logon screen. Except it wasn't a logon screen – with "Username" followed by a blinking cursor. It was a screen asking what *application* I'd like to logon to. Huh?

During those first few months I had a hard time. I'd never heard of Mainframes at university, and yet here they were - and so different from anything I'd ever seen before. There were no courses – just my fellow co-workers trying to help me when they didn't know much more than I did. I was drowning.

Ever since then I've always wondered why there isn't a book that simply and clearly introduces Mainframes. But after trying to write one I now know the answer – because it's really hard! To write a book that isn't fifteen volumes, I've had to simplify things – and there's no doubt that in some cases I've over-simplified. So remember that this is an introduction. If you need more detail then go and check out some of the resources we've given you in Appendix 2.

But by now you've got that first basic understanding of the Mainframe world. You've got a glimpse of what they do, why they're around, and how they're different from other computing systems. You've touched on where the Mainframe comes from, who works on it, and even had a peek at how it all holds together.

You've seen that Mainframes are like that old, dark, forbidding house on the corner you used to be afraid of as a child. The design started out fairly simple but different owners have modified, fixed and added to it as needs have changed. So now it's a vast, complicated mix of things that were needed in the past, things that are needed now, and things to try and get the two to work together. You've also seen that Mainframes do critical back-end tasks and they aren't going anywhere for quite some time.

So now you're ready. You can go on to find out more about Mainframes as you need, or just be able to talk with Mainframe people and have a basic understanding of where they're coming from. But wherever you go from here, good luck in your adventure.

*David Stephens*

# Appendix 1: An Executive Summary - The Whole Book in Three Pages

For those that don't have the time to read the entire book, here's a very, very brief summary

## Chapter 1: What is a Mainframe?
- It's a big computer.
- Almost always an IBM zSeries machine, usually running the z/OS operating system.
- It does lots of work, can have huge databases, and the work and data is often critical.
- It does the 'back end' stuff well. It's more reliable and robust than anything else.
- It doesn't look pretty.
- It's expensive and hard to maintain.

## Chapter 2: Mainframe Hardware
You've got:

- The processor. This can run one or more partitions.
- DASD (disk).

- Tape Drives.
- Printers.

These all talk using *channels* – fiber optic cable.

## Chapter 3: z/OS

Just read the chapter.

## Chapter 4: z/OS Communications

- z/OS gives you two options; SNA (the older one) and TCP/IP (the new one - taking over from SNA).
- Middleware like Websphere MQ and SOAP is very handy for application programs talking to each other.

## Chapter 5: Transaction and Database Managers

- Transaction Managers handle transactions. CICS, Websphere Application Server and IMS are Transaction Managers.
- Database Managers manage databases. DB2, IMS and even CICS are Database Managers.
- You need both.

## Chapter 6: Developing Applications

- You will have applications. Your Mainframe won't do anything you want it to do without them.
- Developing Mainframe applications is a huge task.
- Not only do you need to develop applications, you need to maintain them – also a mammoth task.

## Chapter 7: Mainframe Accessories

- There's lots of software that can run on the Mainframe: monitors, tools, output management, software for a disaster, software to help you process data.
- You'll have a lot of this software.

## Chapter 8: People You Need for a Mainframe
You have:

- Operators.
- Operation Analysts.
- Application Programmers.
- Application Testers.
- Database Administrators.
- Systems Programmers.
- Some others.

You need them all

## Chapter 9: Mainframe Issues

- **Availability**: You don't want your Mainframe crashing or unavailable.
- **Costs**: No surprise here.
- **Software and Hardware Support**: Who do you call when your software or hardware breaks - and will they help you?
- **Disaster Recovery:** What happens if your Mainframe is destroyed?
- **People**: Where to find them?
- **Accounting**: Who in your organization pays for the Mainframe, and how much?
- **Outsourcing**: Do we keep the Mainframe or pay someone else to look after it?
- **Performance**: Why is it taking so long?
- **Capacity Planning**: Planning for upgrades.
- **Environmentals**: Operations room, electricity, etc.
- **Security**: Computer security, physical security.

## The Final Word
You need to read the rest of this book.

# Appendix 2: Where to Go to Next

OK, so where can you find out more? There's an incredible amount of information out there - but it can be hard to find. Here are some of the better resources to get you started.

## IBM Redbooks™

IBM has some great books on Mainframes – and they're free! Go to http://www.redbooks.ibm.com. Some of the best Redbooks are:

- SG24-7333-01 *IBM System z Strengths and Values*.
- SG24-6366 *Introduction to the New Mainframe: z/OS Basics*.
- SG24-7316 *Introduction to the New Mainframe: z/VM Basics*.
- SG24-7436 *Introduction to the New Mainframe: z/VSE Basics*.
- SG24-6772 *Introduction to the New Mainframe: Networking*.
- SG24-6776 *Introduction to the New Mainframe: Security*.
- SG24-7175 *Introduction to the New Mainframe: Large Scale Commercial Computing*.
- SG24-5444 *Introduction to the New Mainframe: Connectivity Handbook*.
- SG24-5352 *IMS Primer*.
- GG24-3376 *TCP/IP Tutorial and Technical Overview* – one of the best introductions to TCP/IP on the market.
- *ABCs of System Programming* – a series of eleven books that go right into z/OS systems administration.

# Manuals

Product manuals are the place to get more technical information, but they can be a bit difficult to read. You can often find manuals online from hardware and software vendors' websites.

For IBM manuals and publications, your starting point is:
http://www.elink.ibmlink.ibm.com/publications/servlet/pbi.wss

Some manuals to look out for include:

- IBM *Introduction to DB2 for z/OS* - a good starting point for DB2 information.

# Other Information on the Web

- http://www.longpelaexpertise.com.au

    Longpela Expertise's website is an excellent place to start for Mainframe information. The website also has a Mainframe-oriented search engine and regular Mainframe articles.

- http://www.Mainframe-upgrade.com
- http://www.wikipedia.org

    Wikipedia® has some great information on Mainframes.

- http://www-03.ibm.com/systems/z/os/zos/zfavorites/

    IBM - they have huge amounts of information. This is your Mainframe starting point.

# Magazines and Articles

- *DBAZine Magazine*

    http://www.dbazine.com

- *Enterprise Systems Journal*

    http://www.esj.com

- *IBM Database Magazine*

  http://www.ibmdatabasemag.com/

- *IBM Hot Topics*

  http://www-03.ibm.com/systems/z/os/zos/bkserv/hot_topics.html

- *IBM Mainframe News*

  http://www-03.ibm.com/systems/z/news/

- *IBM Systems Magazine*
  http://www.ibmsystemsmag.com/Mainframe/

- *Mainframe Executive*

  http://www.Mainframe-exec.com/

- *z/Journal*

  http://www.zjournal.com

## Software Vendors

- ASG

  http://www.asg.com.

- Beta Systems

  http://www.betasystems.com

- Barr Systems

  http://www.barrsystems.com

- BMC

  http://www.bmc.com

- CA

  http://www.ca.com

- Chicago-Soft:

http://www.chicago-soft.com

- Compuware

    http://www.compuware.com

- CSC

    http://www.csc.com

- IBM

    http://www.ibm.com

- InfoPrint

    http://www.infoprintsolutions.com

- LRS

    http://www.levirayshoupe.com

- Macro 4

    http://www.macro4.com

- Merrill Consultants

    http://www.mxg.com

- Micro Focus

    http://www.microfocus.com

- Nexus

    http://www.nexussafe.com

- Oracle

    http://www.oracle.com

- Rocket Software

    http://www.rocketsoftware.com

- Serena

    http://www.serena.com

- Software AG

http://www.softwareag.com

- Syncsort

    http://www.syncsort.com

- SAP

    http://www.sap.com

- Sterling Commerce

    http://www.sterlingcommerce.com

- Tachyon Software

    http://www.tachyonsoft.com

- The SAS Institute

    http://www.sas.com

- TIBCO

    http://www.tibco.com

## Hardware Vendors and Resellers

- HAL Data Services

    http://www.haldata.com.au

- HDS

    http://www.hds.com

- HP

    http://www.hp.com

- IBM

    http://www.ibm.com

- InfoPrint

    http://www.inforprintsolutionscompany.com

- Mainline Information Systems

    http://www.mainline.com

- QSGI

    http://www.qsgi.com

- Sun StorageTek

    http://www.sun.com/storagetek

- Xerox

    http://www.xerox.com

# Appendix 3: Glossary - Translating the Mainframe Speak

Always wanted to know what Mainframe people are talking about? Here's your quick guide. But this is a brief glossary – if you can't find it here, try IBMs website at

http://www.ibm.com/ibm/terminology

**3270** – Terminal used to communicate with a Mainframe. You won't see any today, but anyone using a Mainframe will use 3270 emulation software on their PC - software that pretends to be a 3270 terminal.

**Abend** – Abnormal end. A program crash.

**Address Space** –Environment running under z/OS where programs can run. Every address space looks like an entire z/OS to an application program, and each address space is separated from all the others. You can have hundreds of address spaces running in z/OS. If you're familiar with UNIX or Windows, it's a process.

**Advanced Peer to Peer Network** – SNA network designed for midrange computing systems, but supported by Mainframes.

**AFP** – Advanced Function Presentation. A standard way of printing pretty things on an enterprise printer.

**APAR** - Authorized Program Analysis Report. An official software problem opened by IBM. APARs are fixed with PTFs.

**API** – Application Programming Interface. A way lots of software provides for application programs to use their services. For example, TCP/IP has APIs for programs to use TCP/IP services.

**APPN** – Advanced Peer to Peer Network.

**Application** – One or more programs that does the processing you want. It doesn't do any system related things (like managing hardware or networks) – it performs the processing to suit the needs of your business. You can write your own, or buy one off the shelf.

**Application Program** – A program that is part of your application.

**ASCII** – American Standard Code for Information Interchange. A way of representing characters as numbers for almost all computing platforms in the world – except zSeries Mainframes (which use EBCDIC).

**Assembler** – Programming language. Differs from other high level languages in that you deal more with the physical computer hardware in Assembler. A bit harder to write than other languages but usually runs faster. Mainly used for writing programs that deal with the internals of the computer, or in applications where performance is a big issue.

**ATL** – Automated Tape Library.

**Automated Tape Library** – A tape drive and tape library in one unit. If z/OS wants a particular tape, this unit automatically finds the tape and put it in the correct tape drive.

**Backout** – Undo. You can backout a change to your databases or backout an upgrade to your computer systems.

**Binder** – The z/OS program that creates load modules from object modules.

**Backup** – A spare copy of data that you keep in case something bad happens to the original data.

**Bug** - A problem in a program or software. This can crash the program, make it run slower, or cause it to output something different to what you want.

**Bus and Tag** – Oldest form of Mainframe channel, based on two very thick copper cables. One was the Bus, the other the Tag. Now obsolete.

**C** – A programming language. Relatively new to the Mainframe, but used a lot on UNIX based systems.

**C++** - Expanded C programming language.

**Cache** – Very fast memory in a computer of other hardware. Used to temporarily hold data to improve performance. For example, DASD controllers used cache to hold data that they had already read from disk, in case it is needed again.

**Capacity Planning** – Measuring how busy or full the hardware is, and then planning to handle future capacity increases or decreases.

**Catalog** - Dataset holding the location (i.e. the DASD unit) of a dataset. When you have 1000 or more DASD units, this information becomes really important. A catalog is setup by your Systems Programmer, and is critical to the running of z/OS.

**Change** – A modification to your computing environment. Changing a batch job is a change. Upgrading to a newer Mainframe processor is a change.

**Change Window** – The time period allotted for a change to be implemented. Some changes need an outage to be implemented -

meaning something must be shutdown. So you'll schedule a period of time where this outage can take place – this is your change window. For example, you may have a change window between 0100 and 0130 on Sunday. In this case you must implement or back out that change within this period.

**Channel** – Fast physical connection from the Mainframe to other hardware, such as a Communications Controller or DASD. Only for short distances.

**CICS** – Customer Information Control System. IBM Transaction Manager running on the Mainframe (z/OS, z/VM and z/VSE). It also does some database management tasks.

**Cluster Controller** – Hardware that manages SNA Logical Units. Sometimes called an Establishment Controller.

**COBOL** – **CO**mmon **B**usiness **O**riented **L**anguage. On older programming language, mostly used for commercial applications. A lot of older applications running on the Mainframe are written in COBOL.

**Code** - The actual statements that make up a program. They will be written in a programming language like COBOL or Java.

**Commercial Data Processing** – The work a computer does in the commercial world – basically work with databases. This is the work Mainframes are good at.

**Communications Controller** – Hardware used to manage an SNA network. Sometimes called a Front End Processor or FEP. Now being phased out as TCP/IP becomes the dominant Mainframe network protocol.

**Communication Controller for Linux** – IBM software product that runs on z/Linux and emulates a Communications Controller.

**Composite Application** - An application that spans across different application environments, and sometimes even platforms. A CICS application that accesses data from IMS is a composite application, as is an internet application that accesses a DB2 database.

**Consumables** – Things that are used up. For example, printer consumables include paper and toner – these things are used up by the printer.

**Console** – A terminal that connects directly to the Mainframe. The console is used to control the operating system. You can also have software that emulates (pretends to be) a console.

**Coupling Facility** – Hardware that lets different z/OS operating systems share memory. You need one of these for a Parallel Sysplex.

**Customizing** – Changing to suit your environment. You can customize things like z/OS itself, off the shelf applications, or even hardware.

**DASD** – Direct Access Storage Device. A Mainframe disk.

**DASD Controller** – An older piece of hardware that would sit between DASD and the Mainframe and control the DASD.

**DASD Farm** – A lot of DASD Units in a room. In previous days a large site would have lots and lots of DASD Units in a room. With today's disk devices, huge rooms full of DASD Units are a thing of the past.

**DASD Fast Write** – A facility where a Mainframe sends some data to a DASD controller to be written, but the DASD controller first stores it in cache and signals OK to the Mainframe. The data is actually written later. It improves performance.

**DASD String** –All the DASD sitting behind a DASD Controller.

**Dataset** – Mainframe file.

**DB2** – IBM's relational Database Manager. Runs on the Mainframe and other operating systems like Windows and UNIX.

**DBA** – Database Administrator.

**Develop** - Create. Developing an application means writing the programs to make up an application.

**Developer** - Programmer.

**DFP** – Data Facility Product. Software to manage files and datasets. Part of z/OS. More correctly called DFSMSdfp.

**DFSMS** – Data Facility System Managed Storage. Software that lets you determine on which disk volume newly created datasets will go. This makes creating (or allocating) new datasets easier for users. Part of z/OS. Don't confuse this with DFSMSdss, DFSMSdfp, DFSMShsm or DFSMSrmm - they're separate software products.

**DFW** – DASD Fast Write.

**Disaster Recovery** – Recovering from some disaster that affects your computer.

**Distributed Computer** - A common term for a computer or computer system that isn't a Mainframe.

**Domain** - Part of a shared SNA network that one z/OS controls.

**DR** – Disaster Recovery.


**EBCDIC** – Extended Binary Coded Decimal Interchange Code. A way of representing characters as numbers used by almost no computing platforms except zSeries Mainframes. Other computing platforms use ASCII.

**EE** – Enterprise Extender.

**Emulation Software** – Software that pretends to be something else, such as another computer, piece of hardware, or software. For example, 3270 emulation software pretends to be a 3270 terminal.

**Enterprise Extender** – A way of running SNA inside TCP/IP.

**Enterprise Printer** - A big Mainframe printer. Usually channel connected to a Mainframe, it produces lots and lots of output. They are usually AFP printers.

**Environmentals** - Things needed for a computer room, such as air conditioning, power, physical security, and raised floors.

**EREP** - Environmental Record Editing and Printing. A standard way that z/OS records hardware and software errors.

**ESCON** – Enterprise Systems Connection. A Mainframe channel based on fiber optic cable. ESCON is older than FICON and newer than Bus and Tag.

**Exit** – Code written for an exit point.

**Exit Point** – A point in z/OS and other software where you can write your own code to change things. For example, IMS has an automation exit that sees all IMS system messages. So you could write an exit that does something whenever certain IMS messages are issued.

**FEP** – Front End Processor.

**FICON** – Fiber Connectivity. Newest type of channel, based on fiber optic cable.

**Forward Recovery** - Restore or recovery (for something like a database) where you use journals or logs to perform any changes that have happened since the time of the backup.

**Front End Processor** – Communications Controller.

**Hardware** – Computer equipment you can touch, such as your processor, DASD, or printers.

**HFS** – Hierarchical File System. File system z/OS uses to hold UNIX files – UNIX thinks it's a disk. It is older than zFS.

**High Level Assembler** – Assembler for z/OS.

**HLASM** – High Level Assembler.


**IMS** – IBM Transaction Manager and Database Manager running on the zSeries Mainframe.

**IML** – Initial Microcode Load. Powering on a processor or other hardware equipment with microcode (like a Communications Controller or DASD subsystem).

**In-House** – Doing something yourself rather than buying it or paying someone else to do it. You can write applications in-house, or buy software to do the same thing (if it's available). You can run your Mainframe in-house, or pay an outsourcer to run it for you.

**Initiator** - Address space setup by the Job Entry Subsystem to run batch jobs.

**I/O** - Input/Output. The operation where a processor sends or receives anything to or from external equipment. Reading or writing to disk is I/O, printing is I/O, using a network is I/O.

**IPL** – Initial Program Load. Booting or starting up z/OS (or other Mainframe operating system).

**iSeries** – An IBM midrange computer system. Previously called the IBM AS/400®.

**ISPF** – Interactive System Productivity Facility. Software that comes free with z/OS. It makes TSO/E a little prettier by giving panels or screens, and some standard utilities (like editing a dataset). All TSO/E users use ISPF.

**ISV** - Independent Software Vendor. Third Party Vendor.

**Java – A** programming language mainly used for web applications. New to the Mainframe.

**JCL** – Job Control Language. The language used to create Mainframe batch jobs.

**JES** – Job Entry Subsystem. Software to manage jobs coming in, and output going out with z/OS. You need this to run jobs. It can be JES2 or JES3.

**Keystroke** – A user hitting a key on a keyboard.

**Legacy System** – A computing system that's been around for a long time.

**Link Editor** – Old name for the Binder.

**Lights Out** - Where Operators are not on shift 24 hours a day, seven days a week. This is usually used for sites that have automated operations (without Operators present) performing all operations tasks during certain periods of the day or during weekends. The automation software performs periodic tasks and monitors the systems, automatically notifying support people if there's a problem.

**Load Module** – What a program needs to become before it can run. Programs are usually compiled to produce object files, then put through the Binder to create load modules.

**Logical Partition** – One of the pieces of a PR/SM managed processor. If you use PR/SM to split your physical processor into more than one part that can run an operating system, each part is a Logical Partition.

**Logon** – Gain access to an application or system by passing through a security check – usually by entering your userid and password.

**LU** – SNA Logical Unit. An application or piece of communications hardware, such as a terminal or printer.

**LPAR** – Logical Partition.


**Machine Room** – A room where your computer hardware lives. It is usually climate controlled, secured, and with a raised floor so cables can run underneath it.

**Mainframe** – A big computer. Usually (but not always) referring to IBM's zSeries machines.

**Middleware** - Software that helps applications talk to each other. Websphere MQ and SOAP are middleware.

**Midrange** – A medium sized computer – bigger than a PC, smaller than a Mainframe. For example, the IBM iSeries.

**Migrate** – Move. For example, you can migrate an application programming change from your development environment to production. Or you can migrate a Mainframe application to UNIX.

**Module** - Load module.

**MSU** – Millions of Service Units. A measurement of the size of an operating system image or processor.

**MVS** – Older name for z/OS.

**NCP** – Network Control Program. The IBM software that runs on a Communications Controller or FEP.

**Object Code** – Compiled code. This isn't ready to run yet; it still needs to be passed through the Binder to create a load module.

**Object Module** - Object code.

**Off the Shelf** – Something that is commercially available to buy now. For example, if you buy an application that someone else has written you're buying it 'off the shelf' - like in a supermarket.

**Offsite** – Physically remote from where the Mainframe is.

**On-call** - Being available at any time. For example, a DBA that is on-call will be able to be contacted at any time to solve problems, even if not onsite.

**Onsite** – Physically at the same place (building or location) as the Mainframe.

**Operating System** – The programs that sit between your application programs and the computer hardware. Does things like handle disks, allow more than one application to run at the same time, and clean things up when a program crashes. UNIX and z/OS are both operating systems.

**Operations** – The work done to keep a computer up and running.

**Operations Room** – The room where your computer hardware is, and where your Operators work. Also known as the Machine Room or Computer Room.

**Operator** – The person who operates a computer. Also used to describe the people who monitor Mainframes.

**Ops** - Short for operations.

**OS/390** – Older name for z/OS.

**Outage** – A period where the computer is unavailable. There are two types: scheduled (you planned it – for something like regular maintenance, software upgrades or to implement a change) and unscheduled (you didn't plan it - something's gone wrong).

**Outsourcer** – (Or outsourcing company, or computing bureau) – The company that you pay to run a Mainframe for you. They own and look after your Mainframe, you give them money.

**Panel** – A single computer screen. Traditional 3270 applications send and receive entire screens, or panels.

**Parallel Sysplex** – More than one computer or operating system image talking to each other via a coupling facility. It lets computer systems share information.

**Partitioned Dataset** – A dataset that holds lots of sequential datasets. Similar to a directory.

**Platform** – In Mainframe terms, a computer and operating system. z/OS running on a zSeries computer is a platform. A PC running Windows is another platform.

**PDS** – Partitioned Dataset.

**PL/I** - PL/1.

**PL/1** – Programming Language One. Older programming language, often used in engineering and scientific applications. There are a lot of older applications running on the Mainframe that are written in PL/1.

**Production Environment** – The environment where all the real work is done. The environment can be anything from a batch program or CICS region to an entire data centre. Most organizations will also have a test and/or development environment to test things out before migrating them to their production environment.

**Programmer** - Someone who creates programs by writing them in a programming language.

**PR/SM** - Processor Resource/System Manager. A way for a more than one operating system 'image' to run on one Mainframe processor. You can also use z/VM to do this.

**pSeries** – IBM smaller computer running UNIX. Used to be called an IBM RS/6000®.

**PTF** - Program Temporary Fix. A Mainframe code patch that fixes an error or adds some new functionality. You'd normally install a PTF using SMP/E.

**PU** – SNA Physical Unit. A 'middle man' for SNA networks between LUs.


**QA** - Quality Assurance.

**Quality Assurance Testing** - The testing done on a program after development is complete. This makes sure that there are no bugs before the application is ready for production. Usually done on a completely separate environment - a Quality Assurance environment.


**RACF** – IBM's security software for the Mainframe.

**Recover** - Replace missing or corrupt data with the data from a backup.

**Region** - Address space.

**Restore** – Recover.

**Roll Forward** - After recovering from a backup, using journals or logs to perform changes that have happened to a database since the time of the backup.

Appendix 3: Glossary

**Scratch Tape -** A tape with contents that are no longer needed. This tape can be reused - and the existing contents erased.

**SDLC –** Synchronous Data Link Control. IBM's Communications protocol that allows a Communications Controller to connect with the outside world.

**Sequential Dataset –** Mainframe flat file.

**Server Time Protocol –** A protocol that different operating systems in a Parallel Sysplex use to synchronize their internal clocks.

**Service Level Agreement –** An agreement between a service provider (e.g. the provider of Mainframe services) and a user (e.g. a department or company that uses Mainframe services). In Mainframe terms, a Service Level Agreement is an agreement covering Mainframe services. It will include things like support (e.g. support available 24 hours a day), availability (e.g. Mainframe available during working hours) and response times (e.g. 90% of transactions will have a response time of less than one second).

**Session -** A time where two SNA LUs are connected and talking to each other.

**SLA –** Service Level Agreement.

**SMF –** System Management Facilities. A facility within z/OS that records information such as who's done what, and how long it took. It's often used to record security information for security audits, performance and accounting information.

**SMS –** DFSMS.

**SNA –** Systems Network Architecture. Mainframe networking protocol. Now being superseded by TCP/IP.

**SNI –** SNA Network Interconnect. A way for two different SNA traditional networks to talk to each other.

**SOA** - Service Oriented Architecture. A framework allowing different applications to talk to each other without needing to know where the other application is, what computer it is running on, what language it is written in, or what application environment it uses. Each application is just a service. This lets developers just connect services together to create applications, or at least that's the theory. When people talk about SOA today, they'll usually start talking about SOAP soon after.

**SOAP** - Simple Object Access Protocol. A way of applications talking to each other using standard internet technology: XML and HTTP. People talk about SOA and SOAP hand in hand.

**Software** – Your computer programs, things you can't touch. Operating systems, CICS, and your application programs are all software.

**SPOOL** - A special file maintained by JES that holds batch jobs waiting to run, and input and output for batch jobs.

**STP** – Server Time Protocol.

**Subarea Network** – Traditional SNA network.

**Subsystem** (1) - An entire Application, Transaction or Database Manager. For example, and IMS subsystem would be all the IMS address spaces making up one IMS (control region, MPPs etc.).

**Subsystem** (2) - Program or programs that do operating system related things that normal programs can't do.

**Support** – Assistance that hardware or software vendors provide to ensure their product continues to work – usually for a fee. For example IBM provides support for their hardware; if there's a fault, an engineer will come and fix it. Similarly most Mainframe software has support, so if you find a bug, they'll fix it.

**Sysplex** – Parallel Sysplex.

**Sysplex Timer** – A piece of hardware that different operating systems in a sysplex use to synchronize their internal clocks. Obsolete, and replaced with STP.

**S/360** – System/360. Older computer system that became zSeries.

**S/370** – System/370. Replaced the S/360.

**S/390** – System/390. Replaced the S/370.

**Terminal** – A keyboard and screen used to communicate with a computer.

**TCP/IP** – Networking protocol used by almost all computer systems – especially used for the internet.

**Third Party Vendor** - in Mainframe terms, a vendor who isn't IBM.

**TSO** – TSO/E.

**TSO/E** – Time Sharing Option Extended. A way of using z/OS interactively from a 3270 terminal. Used for maintaining z/OS, and for some applications. It comes free with z/OS.

**Tuning** – Measuring the performance of hardware or software, and then making changes so it performs better.

**Unit Testing** - The testing done on an application program while it's being developed. Once development is complete, another set of testing (Quality Assurance testing) will be done before a program is ready for production.

**UNIX** – An operating system that's almost as old as z/OS. It's used a lot on systems that are smaller than Mainframes, but larger than PCs. Used a lot by computers that deal with the internet. Now available on z/OS.

**UNIX Systems Services** – UNIX interface to z/OS.

**UPS** – Uninterruptible Power Supply. A device that will continue to supply electricity for a short period of time even if the mains power has stopped.

**USS** – UNIX Systems Services.

**Virtualization** - Where multiple operating systems run on the one processor - usually by using hosting software such as z/VM or VMware.

**VSAM** – Virtual Sequential Access Method. A type of dataset – especially good for databases.

**VTAM** – Software running on z/OS that manages SNA networks. Part of IBM Communications Server for z/OS software.

**Web Enable** – Allow users to run an existing program from a web browser. For example, you may have an existing CICS program. If you web enable that program, internet applications can run that program.

**WLM** – Workload Manager.

**Workload Manager** – Software that lets you prioritize work. Important work gets done first, other work gets done if there's enough resources left over.

**zFS** - z/OS file that emulates a UNIX disk. Basically the same as an HFS file, but newer and faster.

**z/Linux** – Linux operating system running on zSeries Mainframes.

**z/OS** – The most popular operating system running on zSeries machine. Previous names include MVS and OS/390.

**zSeries** – an IBM Mainframe. Previous names include System/360, System/370, and System/390.

**z/TPF** – Operating system for the zSeries Mainframe. Not widely used but popular for airline reservation systems.

**z/VM** – Operating system for the zSeries Mainframe. Especially good at hosting other operating systems – a great way of sharing a Mainframe. It is becoming popular with users wanting to run multiple z/Linux images on a zSeries Mainframe.

**z/VSE** – A lesser used operating system for the zSeries Mainframe. Previous names include DOS/VSE.

# Notices

## About This Book
This book is an independent view of the IBM zSeries Mainframe and z/OS operating system. This is not an IBM book. IBM has not contributed to, nor approved of the content of this book.

## Trademarks
The following terms are trademarks of the International Business Machines Corporation in the United States, other countries, or both:

| | | |
|---|---|---|
| Advanced Peer-to-Peer Networking | IMS | QMF |
| | iSeries | Rational |
| AS/400 | Language Environment | Redbooks |
| CICS | | RACF |
| CICS/ESA | MQSeries | REXX |
| CICS/MVS | MVS | RMF |
| CICSPlex | MVS/ESA | RS/6000 |
| ClearCase | MVS/XA | S/360 |
| DB2 | NetView | S/370 |
| DFSMSdfp | OMEGAMON | S/390 |
| DFSMSdss | OS/390 | Sysplex Timer |
| DFSMShsm | pSeries | System/360 |
| DFSORT | Parallel Sysplex | System/370 |
| DOS/VSE | Print Services Facility | System/390 |
| ESCON | | Tivoli |
| FICON | Processor Resource/Systems Manager | VTAM |
| HiperSockets | | WebSphere |
| IBM | PR/SM | z/Architecture |

193

z/OS       z/VSE

z/VM       zSeries

Java, J2EE, Sun, StorageTek, Sun Java, and all Java-based trademarks are trademarks of Sun Microsystems, Inc. in the United States, other countries, or both.

Microsoft, Access, SQL Server, MS-DOS and Windows are trademarks of Microsoft Corporation in the United States, other countries, or both.

UNIX is a registered trademark of The Open Group in the United States and other countries.

Linux is a trademark of Linus Torvalds in the United States, other countries, or both.

APPTUNE, CMF MONITOR, MAINVIEW AUTOOPERATOR, CONTROL-M/ENTERPRISE MANAGER, DASD MANAGER PLUS, APPTune, MAINVIEW TRANSACTION ANALYZER, EVENT MANAGER, CONTROL-M/Tape, and BMC Recovery Manager are trademarks or registered trademarks of BMC Software, Inc. in the United States, other countries, or both.

CA-ACF2, Endevor , MICS, CA-TopSecret, CA Disk, CA-Ops/MVS, CA-1, CA-7, CA-Datacom, CA-IDMS, CA-Ideal, CA–Easytrieve, CA-Librarian, CA-Panvalet, CA-InterTest suite, CA-Verify, CA View, Netmaster, and Unicenter are trademarks of Computer Associates Corporation in the United States, other countries, or both.

Innovation, FDR, ABR, and FDR/Upstream are service marks, trademark and/or registered trademark of INNOVATION Data Processing Corporation in the United States, other countries, or both.

Syncsort is a registered trademark of Syncsort Incorporated.

ASG-Zack, ASG-Zeke, ASG-Existing Systems Workbench (ESW) Suite, ASG-SmartScope, ASG-SmartTune, ASG-SmartTest, TMON, TMON for z/OS, TMON for CICS, TMON for DB2, and TMON for IMS are trademarks of Allen Systems Group, Inc in the United States, other countries, or both.

InfoPrint is a registered trademark of Ricoh Co., Ltd., in the United States, other countries, or both.

Adabas and Natural are trademarks and/or registered trademarks and are Products of Software AG in the United States, other countries, or both.

SAS and SAS/C are trademarks or registered trademarks of SAS Institute Inc. in the United States, other countries, or both.

Micro Focus and Mainframe Express are registered trademarks of Micro Focus Limited in the United States, other countries, or both.

Tachyon Software is a registered trademark and Tachyon Assembler Workbench are trademarks of Tachyon Software in the United States, other countries, or both.

StarTool, ChangeMan and Serena are trademarks of SERENA Software, Inc in the United States, other countries, or both.

Compuware, Abend-AID, File-AID are registered trademarks of Compuware Corporation in the United States, other countries, or both.

Rocket and MAINSTAR are trademarks of Rocket Software, Inc. in the United States, other countries, or both.

EMC and Catalog Solution are trademarks of EMC Corporation in the United States, other countries, or both.

BETA and Harbor are trademarks of Beta Systems Corporation in the United States, other countries, or both.

Connect:Direct is a trademark of Sterling Commerce Inc. in the United States, other countries, or both.

Oracle and PeopleSoft are trademarks or registered trademarks of Oracle Corporation and/or its affiliates

VPS is trademark of Levi, Ray & Shoup, Inc. in the United States, other countries, or both.

SAP is a registered trademark of SAP AG in Germany and in several other countries.

MySQL is a registered trademark of MySQL AB in the United States, the European Union and other countries.

CSC and Hogan are trademarks of Computer Sciences Corporation in the United States, other countries, or both.

Novascale is a trademark of Bull SAS.

Unisys and ClearPath are registered trademarks of Unisys Corporation.

Wikipedia is a registered trademark of the Wikimedia Foundation, Inc.

POSIX is a registered trademark of the IEEE Inc.

Other company, product, or service names may be trademarks or service marks of others.

## Disclaimer

All opinions in this book are the opinions of David Stephens. They do not necessarily represent the view, position or opinion of any other company, organization or person.

Although this book mentions software products by name, it does not necessarily endorse or recommend any products mentioned. Neither David Stephens nor Longpela Expertise has received royalties or payments for the mention of these products.

# Index

## 3

3174. *See* Cluster Controller
3270, 12, 65
3270 emulation, 13
3270 keyboard, 65
3274. *See* Cluster Controller
3380. *See* DASD
3390. *See* DASD
3420, 31
3480, 32
3490, 32
3590, 33
3705. *See* Communications Controller
3725. *See* Communications Controller
3745. *See* Communications Controller
3746. *See* Communications Controller
3880. *See* DASD Controller
3990. *See* DASD Controller

## 9

9 track tape, 31

## A

Acceptance, 114
accountability, 19
accounting, 49
ACID, 89
acronyms, 57
Adabas, 108
Adabas Natural, 111

address space, 46
Advanced Function Printing. *See* AFP
Advanced Peer to Peer Network. *See* APPN
AFP, 37, 62
allocate, 51
Amdahl, Gene, 41
APAR, 116
application, 109
Application Developers, 140
application environment, 91, 110
application program, 110
application server, 91
Application Testers, 141
APPN, 71
archiving datasets, 58
ASCII vs EBCDIC, 52
ASG SmartTune, 124
ASG-SmartScope, 123
ASG-SmartTest, 124
ASG-TMON, 127, 128
ASG-Zack, 61
ASG-Zeke, 62
Assembler. *See* HLASM
ATL. *See* Automated Tape Library
atomic transaction, 90
automated job scheduling, 61
automated operations, 60, 137, 138
Automated Tape Library, 35

## B

backup, 139, 156
backward compatibility, 19
Barr/RJE, 132
batch, 49
batch vs online, 49

BDAM, 52
Beta Systems Harbor, 133
bind, 110
Binder, 112
blackout, 40
blocksize, 51
BMC AppTune, 128
BMC CMF, 59, 132, 154
BMC Control-D, 130
BMC CONTROL-M, 62, 110
BMC CONTROL-M/Tape, 129
BMC CONTROL-T. *See* BMC CONTROL-M/Tape
BMC DASD Advisor, 128
BMC Energizer for CICS, 131
BMC EVENT MANAGER, 129
BMC MAINVIEW, 131
BMC MAINVIEW AUTOOPERATOR, 61
BMC MAINVIEW for Network Management, 128
BMC MAINVIEW TRANSACTION ANALYZER, 129
BMC Recovery Manager, 131
BookManager, 133
brownout, 40
buffering, 48
bus and tag channel, 38
Business Analysts, 113, 146

# C

C, 62, 121
C++, 111
CA, 126
CA Disk, 58
CA NetMaster, 128
CA View, 130
CA-1, 129
CA-7, 62
CA-ACF2, 56
CA-AllFusion, 123
CA-Datacom, 108
CA-Easytrieve, 110, 130

CA-IDMS, 108
CA-Interest, 124
CA-MICS, 132
CA-Ops/MVS, 61
capacity management, 144, 160
capacity planning, 49, *See* capacity management
CA-SORT, 59
CA-TopSecret, 56
CA-Unicenter, 129
CA-Verify, 124
CD, 36
change management, 122, 150
channel, 22, 28, 38, 66
chargeback, 153
chargeout, 153
Chicago-Soft Quick-Ref, 133
CICS, 57, 100, 128, 144
  *AOR, 100*
  *Application Owning Region. See AOR*
  *File Owning Region. See FOR*
  *FOR, 100*
  *Terminal Owning Region. See TOR*
  *TOR, 100*
CICS vs IMS, 105
CICSPlex, 102
CICSPlex Systems Manager. *See* CPSM
Cluster Controller, 65, 67
clustering, 25
COBOL, 62, 97, 103, 111, 121, 123, 155
Codd, Edgar, 97
commercial data processing, 11
Communications Controller, 67, 73, 155
Communications Server, 65
compilers, 62
composite application, 115, 129, 159
Computer Associates. *See* CA
computer room, 40
Compuware AbendAid, 131
Compuware FileAID, 133
Compuware STROBE, 128

concurrent access, 85
console, 54
coupling facility, 25
CPSM, 101, 128
   *CAS, 102*
   *CMAS, 101*
   *MAS, 102*
   *Web User Interface. See WUI*
   *WUI, 102*
CPU. *See* processor
CSC Hogan. *See* Hogan

## D

DASD, 27
DASD cache, 29
DASD Controller, 29
DASD farm, 29
DASD fast write, 30
DASD management, 139, 144
DASD string, 28
data integrity, 19, 82
Database Administrators. *See* DBA
database corruption, 82
database integrity, 82
Database Manager, 81
Datacom. *See* CA-Datacom
dataset, 51
DB2, 98
   *DDF, 98*
   *DRDA, 98*
   *index, 100*
   *IRLM, 98*
   *SPAS, 99*
   *SPUFI, 99*
   *table, 100*
   *tablespace, 100*
   *view, 100*
DB2 Performance Expert, 127
DBA, 86, 100, 137, 142, 144
DBMS. *See* Database Manager
DBRM, 113
DCF, 132
debugging tools, 123
decision support software, 49, 132
DFP, 43

DFSMSdss, 58
DFSMShsm, 58, 131
DFSMSrmm, 129
DFSORT, 59
Disaster Recovery, 86, 147, 152, 157
Disaster Recovery software, 131
disk. *See* DASD
domain, 71
DOS/VSE. *See* z/VSE
DR. *See* Disaster Recovery

## E

EBCDIC vs ASCII, 52
electricity, 40
EMC Catalog Solution, 131
Enterprise Printer, 37
Enterprise Service Bus. *See* ESB
Enterprise Storage Subsystem. *See* ESS
environmentals, 40, 161
EREP, 44, 47
ESB, 79
ESCON, 38
ESS, 30
exits, 54, 144
extents, 51

## F

Fault Analyzer, 131
FEP. *See* Communications Controller
FICON, 39
File Manager, 133
footprint, 23
forward recovery, 85, 104
Front End Processor. *See* Communications Controller

## G

generator, 40
Global Resource Sharing. *See* GRS
GRS, 26

199

## H

hardware support, 14
help desk, 119, 146
Hercules, 155
hierarchical database, 95
High Level Assembler. *See* HLASM
HiperSockets, 73
HLASM, 44, 103, 111, 121
Hogan, 110
HP, 30
HTTP Server, 44, 107

## I

IBM CICS VSAM Recovery, 104
IBM HLASM Toolkit, 123
IBM RMDS, 130
IBM TPNS, 124
ICFRU, 131
IDMS. *See* CA-IDMS
IMS, 57, 92, 127, 144
   *BMP, 93*
   *CQS, 94*
   *DB/DC, 92*
   *DBB, 93*
   *DBCTL, 92*
   *DBRC, 93*
   *DCCTL, 92*
   *DL/I, 93, 95*
   *DLISAS, 93*
   *Fastpath, 93, 95*
   *FDBR, 94*
   *IFP, 93*
   *IRLM, 94*
   *JBP, 93*
   *JMP, 93*
   *MPP, 93*
   *OM, 94*
   *Online Image Copy, 96*
   *RECON, 93*
   *RM, 94*
   *SCI, 94*
   *TM/DB, 92*
IMS Connect, 94
IMS vs CICS, 105
IMSPlex, 94
InfoMan, 133
InfoPrint Page Printing Formatting Aid, 132
InfoPrint XML Extender for z/OS, 132
Initial Program Load. *See* IPL
initiator, 50
Innovation ABR, 58, 131
Innovation FDR, 58
Innovation FDR/Upstream, 133
IPL, 23
ISPF, 44, 53
ISV, 127
ITCAM, 129

## J

Java, 53, 62, 97, 103, 111, 121
JCL, 51, 110
JES. *See* Job Entry Subsystem
JES2, 44, 51
JES3, 44, 51
JES328X, 62
job, 49, 130
Job Control Language. *See* JCL
Job Entry Subsystem, 49
job schedule, 138
job scheduling, 61
job step, 50
journaling, 102

## L

Language Environment, 44, 118
LE. *See* Language Environment
legacy system, 12, 16
lights out, 137
link-edit, 110
load module, 111
logging, 102
Logical Unit. *See* LU

LPAR, 23
LU, 69

## M

Macro4 Expetune, 123
mainframe, 11
mediation, 79
message mediation, 79
message routing, 79
MicroFocus Mainframe Express, 122
middleware, 76
Millions of Service Units. *See* MSU
monitoring software, 125
MQ Series. *See* Websphere MQ
MSU, 154
MVS/ESA, 44
MVS/SP, 44
MVS/XA, 44
MXG, 132

## N

NetView, 110, 128
network layers, 66
network printer, 37
Nexus MEMO, 133

## O

object code, 110
online vs batch, 49
Open Systems Integration. *See* OSI
operating system, 43
Operations Analyst, 138, 146
Operator, 40, 54, 135, 139, 150
Oracle PeopleSoft. *See* PeopleSoft
OS/390, 44
OS/VS2, 44
OSA Express, 72
OSI, 69
output management software, 130
outsourcing, 158

## P

panel, 53
Parallel Channel, 38
Parallel Sysplex, 24, 30, 33, 101
Partitioned Dataset. *See* PDS
PDS, 52
PDSE, 52
PeopleSoft, 110
performance, 159
performance monitoring, 49
performance tools, 123
Physical Unit, 69
PL/1, 97, 103, 121
PR/SM, 22, 23
Print Services Facility. *See* PSF
printer, 37
printing, 62
printing software, 132
processor, 22
Processor Resource/Systems Manager. *See* PR/SM
PSF, 62
PTF, 116
PU. *See* Physical Unit

## Q

QA, 114
QMF, 100
Quality Assurance. *See* QA
Query Management Facility. *See* QMF

## R

RACF, 56
RAID, 28
Rational Application Developer, 122
redundancy, 24
refurbished mainframes, 27
relational database, 95
reliability, 19
remote copy, 157
reporting tools, 130
REXX, 110

201

RMF, 59, 132, 154
Rocket MAINSTAR, 128
rolling back, 84
runtime environment, 118

## S

SAP, 110
SAS, 110, 130
SAS/C, 111
scratch tape, 34
screen scraping, 70
SDLC, 67
second hand mainframes, 27
security, 161
security software, 56, 144
Securty Administrators, 139
sequential dataset, 51
Serena ChangeMan, 122
Serena StarTool, 122
Serena StarToolFDM, 133
Server Time Protocol, 27
Service Level Agreement. *See* SLA
Service Oriented Architecture. See SOA
Share, 138
shift, 136
Side Boxes
   *A Program to Install Programs - SMP/E*, 60
   *A Serviced Office for your Programs - Language Environment*, 118
   *ASCII and EBCDIC*, 52
   *Codd and the Birth of Relational Databases*, 97
   *Confused Over CICS?*, 103
   *Database and Transaction Managers on Other Platforms*, 85
   *Deciphering the IBM Hardware Code*, 32
   *Doing it Better Than IBM - Gene Amdahl*, 41

*Hercules - A Mainframe on Your PC*, 155
*How Many COBOLs Are There?*, 123
*IBM as Snow White?*, 16
*Mainframe Software Costs - Pay for What You Use*, 154
*Mainframe Software Support*, 116
*Online and Batch*, 49
*Screen Scraping*, 70
*Share - Mainframe School?*, 138
*The American Dream - Charles Wang and Computer Associates*, 126
*The Mainframe Secret Code - Acronyms*, 57
*The Many Names of z/OS*, 44
*The Oldest Box in the Room*, 73
*The Other SNA*, 71
*The Second Hand Mainframe Market*, 27
*The Shortage of Mainframe People*, 145
*The Y2K 'Bug'*, 17
*TN3270 - Today's Window to the Mainframe*, 72
*Transactions and the ACID Test*, 89
*What Else Can Run on a Mainframe?*, 63
*What is a Started Task?*, 54
*What is an Operating System?*, 45
*What is Websphere?*, 106
*What's a Network?*, 69
*What's a Terminal?*, 67
*What's a Transaction?*, 84
*What's an IMSPlex?*, 94
*What's RAID?*, 30
*Where Did The Third Party Vendors Go?*, 127
*Why Are Mainframes Using Older Technology?*, 19

*Why Have IMS AND CICS?*, 105
*Your Shrinking Need for Mainframe People*, 142
*Your Three Application Environments*, 114
*zIIPs and zAAPs*, 25
Simple Object Access Protocol. *See* SOAP
SLA, 159
SMF, 48, 57, 59, 154
SMP/E, 44, 60
SNA, 43, 65, 145, 155
SNA Network Interconnect. *See* SNI
SNA vs TCP/IP, 74
SNI, 71
SOA, 76
SOAP, 78, 97, 103, 108
software licensing, 14
software support, 116, 117
sorting, 58
speciality processor, 25
spool, 50
SPUFI. *See* DB2 SPUFI
SQL, 99
SSCP, 70
started task, 54, 130
STC. *See* started task
Sterling Commerce Connect Direct, 132
StorageTek, 36
stored procedure, 99
STP. *See* Server Time Protocol
stress test, 124
subarea network, 67
sub-capacity pricing, 154
Sun StorageTek. *See* StorageTek
Sun StorageTek 9990V, 29
SyncSort, 59
sysplex. *See* Parallel Sysplex
Sysplex Timer, 27
System Management Facilities. *See* SMF
System z New Application License Charge. *See* zNALC
System/360, 19
System/370, 10

System/390, 10
Systems Automation, 61
Systems Network Architecture. *See* SNA
systems performance, 144
Systems Programmer, 47, 54, 137, 143, 151, 152, 156, 160

# T

Tachyon Assembler Workbench, 122
tape, 31
tape compatibility, 36
Tape Librarian, 34
tape library, 34
tape management software, 35, 129
tape mount, 35
TCO, 153
TCP/IP, 43, 72, 145, 156
TCP/IP vs SNA, 74
TDS. *See* Tivoli Decision Support
terminal, 12, 65
terminal emulator, 65
test tools, 124
testcases, 124
TIBCO Enterprise Message Service, 80
Tivoli Composite Application Manager. *See* ITCAM
Tivoli Decision Support, 132
Tivoli Monitoring, 129
Tivoli OMEGAMON, 126
Tivoli Workload Scheduler, 62
TN3270, 72
total cost of ownership. *See* TCO
TP. *See* transaction processor
TPF. *See* z/TPF
transaction, 82, 84
Transaction Manager, 87
transaction processor, 91
TSO. *See* TSO/E
TSO/E, 44, 53, 54, 99, 102, 110, 111, 139, 144
TWS. *See* Tivoli Workload Scheduler

203

## U

Uninterruptible Power Supply. *See* UPS
UNIX, 15
UNIX System Services. *See* USS
UPS, 40, 156
used mainframes, 27
USS, 43, 52, 112, 144

## V

virtualization, 24
VMware, 24
Volume Serial Number, 28, 36, 51
VPS, 62
VSAM, 52, 100, 104

## W

Wang, Charles, 126
web services, 107
Websphere Application Server. *See* Websphere AS
Websphere AS, 105
Websphere Developer, 122
Websphere Enterprise Service Bus, 80
Websphere MQ, 77
WLM, 47
Workload Manager. *See* WLM

## X

Xerox, 38
Xerox DocuPrint, 38

## Y

Y2K Bug, 17
Year 2000. *See* Y2K Bug

## Z

z/Linux, 63
z/OSe, 44
z/TPF, 63
z/VM, 24, 63
z/VSE, 63
zAAP, 25
zFS, 52
zIIP, 25
zNALC, 44

# Table of Figures

Figure 1: A 3270 Mainframe Screen (courtesy Jolly Giant Software).......13
Figure 2: Mainframe Setup Example with Two Processors......................22
Figure 3: IBM z990 Processor (courtesy of IBM Archives).......................23
Figure 4: Mainframe DASD String...............................................................28
Figure 5: DASD Farm (courtesy of IBM Archives).....................................28
Figure 6: Sun StorageTek 9990V Disk Subsystem (courtesy of Sun StorageTek)....................................................................................................29
Figure 7: 3420 (reel) and 3480 (cartridge) Tapes (courtesy of IBM Archives)......................................................................................................33
Figure 8: Sun StorageTek SL8500 ATL (courtesy of Sun StorageTek).......35
Figure 9: Xerox DocuPrint 525 Enterprise Printer (courtesy of Xerox)....38
Figure 10: Parallel Channel Cable (courtesy Patrick Finnegan and www.computer-refuge.org)........................................................................39
Figure 11: Operating System Functions Inside and Outside of z/OS..........55
Figure 12: A 3270 Style Keyboard..............................................................66
Figure 13: Example of a Traditional SNA Network...................................68
Figure 14: A Mainframe TCP/IP Network..................................................74
Figure 15: Websphere MQ..........................................................................77
Figure 16: An IMS Subsystem....................................................................92
Figure 17: IMS and IMS Supporting Address Spaces................................95
Figure 18: A DB2 Subsystem......................................................................99
Figure 19: Connected CICS Regions........................................................101
Figure 20: A CICSPlex...............................................................................102
Figure 21: Websphere Application Server Setup.....................................107

# About the Author

David Stephens saw his first Mainframe in 1989, and can't seem to get away from them. After graduating with an Engineering degree from the University of Tasmania, he spent six months working as a Mainframe Network Operator before moving to z/OS Systems Programmer. Since then David has amassed over seventeen years of Mainframe technical experience - working on almost every aspect of managing and operating Mainframes. He also has six years experience working in Systems Software Development and Level 3 Software Support for IBM.

When not working on Mainframes, David loves to travel the world, go walking for days in the wilderness, scuba dive, or some combination of these. He'll also happily drink your red wine collection dry.

David currently works as a Systems Programmer Consultant with Longpela Expertise. He lives in Perth, Western Australia.